Praise for
Leadership by Algorithm

"Everyone is talking about artificial intelligence, but no one has a clue how it will affect the way organizations are managed... until now. David De Cremer, a leading expert, has written the most informative book I've read on how algorithms will change leadership—and which parts are unlikely to be replaced by a machine."

Adam Grant, *New York Times* bestselling author of *Originals* and *Give and Take*, and host of the chart-topping TED podcast *WorkLife*

"Will your next boss be a robot? In case you haven't pondered your AI future, David De Cremer—one of the 'World's Top 30 Management Gurus'—has done it for you in his fascinating book, Leadership By Algorithm. *Read your future today."*

James Bradley, three-times *New York Times* bestseller and author of *Flags of Our Fathers*

"David De Cremer, one of the top gurus in corporate culture, provides unique insight in Leadership by Algorithm *as to what leadership means in the AI age. Ignore at your peril!"*

Alexandros Papaspyridis, Director Higher Education at Microsoft Asia Pacific Japan

"Leadership by Algorithm *is extremely topical, and can give us guidance on how to redefine leadership for the next decade.*"

Peter Hinssen, serial technology entrepreneur and author of *The New Normal* and *The Day After Tomorrow*

"*David De Cremer addresses the weighty topic of the appropriate organizational roles for AI and algorithms in a way that is lucid, accessible, and thought provoking. AI plays an increasingly vital part in the functioning of business and society. As this book points out, true leaders need to consider, thoughtfully, the associated opportunities and risks to respond in a way that is genuinely wise, not merely clever.*"

Robert Koepp, Principal of Geoeconomix and former director of The Economist Group

"*The business world moves in fast and volatile ways, which requires companies today to augment human intelligence by employing artificial intelligence systems. But, how to do this? In* Leadership by Algorithm, *David De Cremer addresses this question and introduces you to a whole new way of thinking about the role that algorithms will and should play in organizations to win. Highly recommended!*"

Alex Schenk, Head FRA Operations Novartis Business Services

"*In our rapidly technologizing times, AI may be blazing a trail but sound leadership is essential for harnessing its full potential.* Leadership by Algorithm *provides powerful insights for riding this critical wave.*"

Sun Sun Lim, author of *Transcendent Parenting: Raising Children in the Digital Age* and Professor and Head of Humanities, Arts and Social Sciences, Singapore University of Technology and Design

"*Like the long-discussed dispute over efficiency and equality, the rapid development of AI gives rise to the discussion whether the pursuit of maximizing efficiency at the cost of a less humane society is acceptable?* Leadership by Algorithm *echoes the importance of using AI in wise ways to improve the human condition—a purpose that technology is originally developed to serve. Thought-provoking!*"

Frederick Shen, CIO, Aeternam Stella Investment Group

LEADERSHIP
by
ALGORITHM

Every owner of a physical copy of this edition of

LEADERSHIP
by
ALGORITHM

can download the eBook for free direct from us at Harriman House, in a DRM-free format that can be read on any eReader, tablet or smartphone.

Simply head to:

ebooks.harriman-house.com/
Leadershipbyalgorithm

to get your copy now.

LEADERSHIP
by
ALGORITHM

Who leads and who follows
in the AI era?

DAVID DE CREMER

First published in 2020 by Harriman House Ltd

3 Viceroy Court
Bedford Road
Petersfield
Hampshire
GU32 3LJ
GREAT BRITAIN
Tel: +44 (0)1730 233870

Email: enquiries@harriman-house.com
Website: www.harriman-house.com

Paperback ISBN: 978-0-85719-828-0
eBook ISBN: 978-0-85719-829-7

British Library Cataloguing in Publication Data
A CIP catalogue record for this book can be obtained from the British Library.

For Hannah
– with the aspiration for her
to live an authentic life in a
nearly automated future!

Contents

Prologue

I'M SEATED AT a round table where I am being introduced to several conference attendees. Our table is not the only one in the room. Many other round tables fill up the ballroom and have people seated in nice suits and dresses. After being introduced to my neighbors, I sit down and look around for a moment to make myself familiar with the context.

It is 7pm on a Thursday evening. I am a young scholar, only having received my PhD a few years ago, and I find myself in the midst of a fancy business event. When I was invited by a colleague, I was unsure about whether to go, not knowing how it could be relevant for my research. Did I have anything in common with these executives? It took some persuasion, but eventually my colleague convinced me and here I was. So, to make the best out of it, I started talking to my neighbor.

He was a young, ambitious person, who seemed to have it all figured out. He was recently promoted to an executive position and had a clear idea about what success was and how to achieve it. Clearly someone who knew what he was doing. I became intrigued with his acute drive to talk about his successes and his conviction that you have to push limits until you get what you want.

After listening for a while, I managed to ask him a question. My question, which must have sounded quite naïve to those sitting at my table, was how he was so convinced that a business world where everyone would be pushing the limits continuously could survive. Wouldn't it be the case that such behavior, shown by all, would create problems and maybe damage or even destroy the system that had been built?

As I expected, he was surprised, and for a second it almost looked like he didn't know what to say. However, he quickly overcame his surprise and simply responded that such a situation would never happen. If there was any risk that our behavior would lead to threats to our organizations or society, he was convinced that science and technology would solve it. In his view, technology allowed us to push beyond our human limits and helped to overcome any challenges that we may encounter.

Somewhat taken by his answer, I followed up with another question, asking him whether such a belief in the almost *superpower* of technology would not make him too dependent on that same technology. Wouldn't that make him surplus to requirements in the long term? He looked at me in disbelief and said with a grin on his face that I should not worry about that, because it would never be an issue. He then turned his attention to the neighbor on his other side, which made clear to me that our conversation was finished.

As a young scholar, but also as a person, this conversation made a deep impression on me. The story stayed with me for many years, but eventually I forgot about it. Until a few years ago! When I started working on questions addressing the existential drive of humans in developing technology the story came back to me. And, this time, two thoughts kept flashing through my head.

First, why was it that my companion at the dinner didn't seem to be aware that his own behavior was leading to problems that could only be solved if the science of technology made sufficient progress? Second, where did he find that sense of confidence that technology would solve it all for him to remain in charge and to keep doing what he was doing?

Both questions are important to ask, but I was particularly intrigued by the thought that someone could be so confident in technology innovation. It made me curious as to the kind of future that awaits us when technology will have the potential to impact on our lives in such a significant way. What kind of technology would that be and how would it affect us?

Well, as you are probably all aware, today we are living in an era where exactly this kind of technology innovation is knocking loudly on all of our doors. It is a strong and confident knock from a technology ready to take its place in human society. What am I talking about? Clearly, I am talking about artificial intelligence (AI).

Today, AI is beyond cool! Every advancement that is made in the field of technology is hailed as a great triumph by many. And with that triumph its impact becomes visible and that impact is recognized as significant. Indeed, AI brings the message that our world will change fundamentally.

In a sense, the rapid development of AI and its many applications gives us a peek into a future where our society will function in a completely different way. With the arrival of AI, we can already see a future in place that forces all of us to act now. AI is the kind of technology innovation that is so disruptive that if you do not start changing your ways of working today, there may not even be a future for you tomorrow.

While this may come across as somewhat threatening, it is a future that we have to be serious about. If Moore's law – the idea that the overall processing power of computers will double every two years – is applicable, then in the next decade we should be ready to witness dramatic changes in how we live and work together. All of this buzz has made me – just as when I met the very ambitious executive – curious about a technology-driven future. For me, AI is acting as a time machine, helping us to see what could be, but at a moment in time that we actually still have to build it. And, this is an interesting thought.

Why?

Well, if we consider AI as a kind of time machine, giving us a peek into the future, we should use it to our benefit. Use it in a way that can help us to be conscious and careful about how we design, develop and apply AI. Because once the future sets in, the past may be remembered, but it will be gone.

Today, we still live in a time where we can have an impact on technology. Why am I saying this? Let me respond to this question by referring to a series on Netflix that I very much enjoyed watching. The series is called *Timeless* and describes the adventures of a team that wants to stop a mysterious organization, called Rittenhouse, from changing history by making use of a time machine.

In the first episode, the relevance to our discussion in this book is obvious right away. There, one of the main characters, Lucy Preston, a history professor, is introduced to Connor Mason, who is the inventor of a time machine. Mason explains that certain individuals have taken control of a time machine, called the Lifeboat, and gone back in time. With a certain weight in his voice, he makes clear that "history will change". Everyone in the room is aware of the magnitude of his words and realizes the consequences that this will have on the world, society and maybe even their own lives.

Lucy Preston responds emotionally by asking why he would be so stupid as to invent something so dangerous. Why invent technology that could hurt the human race in such significant ways (i.e. changing its own history)? The answer from Mason is as clear as it is simple: he didn't count on this happening. And, isn't this how it usually goes with significant technological innovations? Blinded by the endless opportunities, we don't want to waste any time and only look at what technology may be capable of. The consequences of an unchecked technology revolution for humanity are usually not addressed.

Can we expect the same thing with AI? Are we fully aware of the implications for humanity if society becomes smart and automated? Are we focusing too much on developing a human-like intelligence that can surpass real human intelligence in both specific and general ways? And, are we doing so without fully considering the development and application dangers of AI?

As with every significant change, there are pros and cons. Not too long ago, I attended a debate where the prospects of a smart society were discussed. Initially the focus was entirely on the cost recommendations and efficiencies that AI applications would bring. Everyone was happy so far.

At one point in the debate, however, someone in the audience asked whether we shouldn't evaluate AI more critically in terms of its functionality for us as human beings, rather than on maximizing the abilities of the technology itself. One speaker responded loudly with the comment that AI should definitely tackle humanity's problems (e.g. climate change, population size, food scarcity and so forth), but its development should not be slowed down by anticipatory thoughts on how it would impact humanity itself. As you can imagine, the debate became suddenly much more heated. Two camps formed relatively quickly. One camp advocated a focus on a race to the bottom to maximize AI abilities as fast as possible (and thus discounting long-term consequences for humanity), whereas the other camp advocated the necessity of social responsibility in favor of maximizing technology employment.

Who is right? In my view, both perspectives make sense. On the one hand, we do want to have the best technology and maximize its effectiveness. On the other hand, we also want to ensure that the technology being developed will serve humanity in its existence, rather than potentially undermining it.

So, how to solve this dilemma?

In this book, I want to delve deeper into this question and see how it may impact the way we run our teams, institutes and organizations, and what the choices will be that we have to make. It is my belief that in order to address the question of how to proceed in the development and application of algorithms in our daily activities, we need to agree on the purpose of the technology development itself. What purpose does AI serve for humanity and how will this impact the shaping of it? This kind of exercise is necessary to avoid two possible outcomes that I have been thinking about for years.

First, we do not want to run the risk that the rapid development of AI technologies creates a future where our human identity is slowly removed and a humane society becomes something of the past. Like Connor Mason's time machine that altered human history, mindless development of AI technology, with little awareness of its consequences for humanity, may run the same risks.

Second, we push the limits of technology advancement with the aim for AI to augment our abilities and thus to serve the development of a more (and not less) humane society. From that point of view, the development of AI should not be seen as a way to solve the mess we create today, but rather as a means of creating opportunities that will improve the human condition. As the executive I met as a young scholar proclaimed that technology is developed to deal with the problems that we create, AI technology developed with the sole aim of maximizing efficiency and minimizing errors will reduce the human presence rather than augment its ability.

Putting these two possible outcomes together made me realize that the purpose served by investing so much in AI technology advancement should not be to make our society less humane and more efficient in eliminating mistakes and failures. This would result in humankind having to remove itself from its place in the world to be replaced by another type of intelligence not burdened by human flaws. If this were to happen, our organizations and society would ultimately be run by technology. What will our place in society be then?

In this book, I will address these questions by unravelling the complex relationship that exists between on the one hand our human desire to constantly evolve, and the drive for fairness and co-operation on the other hand. Humans have an innate motivation to go where no man has gone before. The risk associated with this motivation is that at some point we may lose control of the technology we are building and the consequence will be that we will submit to it.

Will this ever be a reality? Humans as subordinates of the almighty machine? Some signs indicate that it may well happen. Take the example of the South Korean Lee Sedol, who was the world champion at the ancient Chinese board game Go. This board game is highly complex and was considered for a long time beyond the reach of machines. All that changed in 2016 when the computer program AlphaGO beat Lee Sedol four matches to one. The loss against AI made him doubt his own (human) qualities so much that he decided to retire in 2019. So, if even the world champion admits defeat, why would we not expect that one day machines will develop to the point where they run our organizations?

To tackle this question, I will start from the premise that the leadership we need in a humane society is likely not to emerge through more sophisticated technology. Rather, enlightened leadership will emerge by becoming more sophisticated about human nature and our own unique abilities to design better technology that is used in wise (and not smart) ways.

Let me take you on a journey, where we will look at what exactly is happening today with AI in our organizations; what we can expect from moving into a new era where algorithms are developed for each task; what kind of influence it will have on how we will run our organizations in the future; and how we should best approach such radical transformation.

The time machine is waiting, but this time with the aim to inform us and make us smarter about the ways in which we can design technology to improve humanity.

CHAPTER I
Entering a New Era

I N 1985, MARK Knopfler and his band Dire Straits released a song about a boy who got the action, got the motion and did the walk of life. This boy became the hero in many a young kid's fantasy. In the 21st century, we have another kind of hero, something that is not human. Now, we admire the use of algorithms in all walks of life.

However, it is also important to note that AI is not some new phenomenon that has only arrived in the last few years. In fact, the notion of AI was used for the first time in 1956. At that time, the eight-week long Dartmouth Summer Research project on AI at Dartmouth College in New Hampshire was organized. The project included names like Marvin Minsky, John McCarthy and Nathaniel Rochester, who would later become known as the founding fathers of AI.

So, early on in the second half of last century, the belief in the super power of AI was already very much present. Consider, for example, the quote of Herbert A. Simon, Nobel laureate in economics, who wrote in 1965: "machines will be capable, within 20 years, of doing any work a man can do." However, researchers failed to deliver on these lofty promises. Since the 1970s, AI projects have been heavily criticized for being too expensive and using too formalized, top-down approaches which fail to replicate human intelligence. And as a result, AI research was partly frozen, with no real progress being made. Until now!

AI witnessed a comeback in the last decade, primarily because the world woke up to the realization that deep learning by machines is possible to the level where they can actually perform many tasks better than humans. Where did this wake-up call come from? From a simple game called Go.

In 2016, AlphaGo, a program developed by Google DeepMind, beat the human world champion in the Chinese board game, Go. This was a surprise to many, as Go – because of its complexity – was considered the territory of human, not AI, victors. In a decade where our human desire to connect globally, execute tasks faster, and accumulate massive amounts of data, was omnipresent, such deep learning capabilities were, of course, quickly embraced.

As a result, we are now witnessing an almost obsessive focus on AI and the benefits it can bring to our society, organizations and people. This obsessive focus, combined with an exponential increase in AI applications, has resulted in a certain fear that human intelligence may well be on the verge of being challenged in all facets of our lives. Or, to be more precise, a fear has emerged in society that we, as humans, may have entered an era where we will be replaced by machines (for real, this time!).

However, before we address the challenge (some may even call it a threat) to our authentic sense of the human self and intelligence, we need to make clear what we are talking about when we talk about AI. Although the purpose of this book is not to present a technical manual to work with AI, or to teach you how to become a coder, I do feel that we first need to familiarize ourselves with a brief definition of AI.

In its simplest form, AI can be seen as a system that employs techniques to make external data – available everywhere in our organizations and society – as a whole more transparent. Making data more transparent allows for interpreting data more accurately. This allows us to learn from these interpretations and subsequently act upon them to promote more optimal ways of achieving our goals.

The technique that is known to all and drives our learning from data is called machine learning. It is machine learning that creates algorithms that are applied to data with the aim of promoting our understanding of what the data is actually saying. Algorithms are learned scripts for mathematical calculations that are applied to data to arrive at new insights and conclusions that we may not directly see. Specifically, they allow us to arrive at insights that can help us to develop more comprehensive and more accurate predictions and models. Algorithms act in autonomous ways to identify patterns in data that signal underlying principles and rules.

As you can easily see, algorithms are not only useful but powerful tools in a society interested in continuously improving and enhancing knowledge. Indeed, algorithms are en route to serve such an important function to how we act and live in society that they will be as much part of our *social* and *work* lives as other human beings. In other words, the ability of algorithms to analyze, work with and learn from external data, means that algorithms today have reached a level where they can interact and partner with the outside (human) world.

The rise of algorithms in organizations

When you look around today and see what excites people about the future, it quickly becomes clear that the influence of our new hero (the algorithm in action) is rapidly growing, especially in domains where the potential for realizing significant cost savings is high. One such domain concerns our work life, where algorithms are increasingly becoming part of how organizations are managed.[1] Although it may be a scary development for some of us, there are good reasons why algorithms are applied to a wide variety of problem-solving operations.[2]

Let us first look at the economic benefits. Current estimates show that the application of AI in business will add at least $13trn to the global economy in the next ten years. In a recent report by PwC, it was predicted that using AI at a larger scale – across industries and society – could boost the global economy by $15.7trn by 2030.[3,4]

Why do we expect AI to contribute in such enormous ways to the global economy? Mainly because algorithms are expected to have an impact on how businesses will be managed and controlled (as indicated by 56% of interviewed managers by Accenture) and therefore will facilitate the creation of a more interesting and effective work context (as indicated by 84% of managers interviewed by Accenture).[5,6] This enhancement in effectiveness will ensure economic growth. Indeed, surveys worldwide indicate that the adoption of algorithms in the work context will help businesses to promote the fulfilment of their potential and create larger market shares.[7,8]

For some, these numbers have been used to suggest that algorithms represent steroids for companies wanting to perform better and faster. It is nevertheless a reality that companies today are developing new partnerships between machines and AI on one hand, and humans on the other hand. Developing and promoting this kind of partnership also has an important implication for humankind. It is likely that the new technology, available to push companies' productivity and performance to a higher level, is bound to steadily take more autonomous forms that will enable humans to offload parts of their jobs. Importantly, this development is not something that is likely to happen tomorrow. In fact, it has arrived already. AI is developing so fast that an increasing number of machines are already capable of autonomous learning. In reality, AI has achieved a level of development that makes it capable of taking actions and making decisions that previously were only considered possible under the discretion of humans.

If this is the case, then it is no surprise that the availability and possibility of implementing intelligent machines and their learning algorithms will have a significant impact on how work will be executed and experienced. This reality is hard to deny because the facts seem to be there. As mentioned earlier, Google's DeepMind autonomous AI beat the world's best Go-player, and recently Alibaba's algorithms have been shown to be superior to humans in the basic skills of reading and comprehension.[9]

If such basic human skills can be left to machines and those machines possess the ability to learn, what then will the future look like? This predicted (and feared?) change in the nature of work will be seen across a broad range of jobs and professions. It is already widely accepted that automation of jobs in the business world is happening. For example, algorithms are being employed to recruit new staff, decide which employees to promote, and manage a wide range of administrative tasks.[10,11,12]

But companies are not just investing in complex algorithms for passive administrative tasks that can lead to hiring the best employees. They are also being used already for more active approaches. For example, the bank JPMorgan Chase uses algorithms to track employees and assess whether or not they act in line with the company's compliance regulations.[13] Organizations thus see the benefit of algorithms in the daily activities of their employees.

As another case in point, companies have set out to enable algorithms to track how satisfied employees feel, in order to predict the probability of them resigning. For any organization this type of data is important and useful in promoting effective management. After all, once the right kind of people are working in the organization, you want to do all you can to keep them. In that respect, an interesting study from the US National Bureau of Economic Research demonstrated that low-skill service-sector workers (where retention rates are low) stayed in the job 15% longer when an algorithm was used to judge their employability.[14]

Automation and innovation

Automation and the corresponding use of algorithms with deep learning abilities are also penetrating other industries. The legal sector is another area where many discussions are taking place about how and whether to automate services. Legal counsellors have started to use automated advisors to contest relatively small fines such as parking tickets.

The legal sector is also considering the use of AI to help judges go through evidence collected to reach a verdict in court cases. Here, algorithms are expected to help present evidence needed to make decisions where the interests of different stakeholders are involved. The fact that decisions, including the interests of different stakeholders, may become automated should make us aware that automation in the legal sector introduces risks and challenges. Indeed, such use of algorithms may put autonomous learning machines well on the way to influencing *fair* decisions within the framework of the law. Needless to say, if questions about human rights and duties gradually become automated, we will enter a potentially risky era where human values and priorities could become challenged.

Another important industry where technology and the use of automated learning machines are quickly becoming part of the ecosystem is financial services. Traders and those running financial and risk management are working in an environment where digital adoption and machine learning are no longer the exception.[15] Rather, in today's financial industry, they seem to have become the default. In fact, the use and application of algorithms to, for example, manage risk analysis or provide personalized products based on the profile of the customer is unparalleled. It has reached the level where we can confidently say that banks today are technology companies first, and financial institutes second. It's no surprise that the financial industry is forecast to spend nearly $300bn in 2021 on IT, up from about $260bn just three years earlier.[16]

It is not only that banks have embraced technology so much that it has transformed the workings of their industry significantly. No, it is also the other way around. Technology companies are now moving into the financial industry. Indeed, tech companies are becoming banks. Take recent examples such as Alibaba (BABA), Facebook (FB), and Amazon (AMZN); all are moving into providing financial services and products.

A final important area where we see that the use of autonomous learning algorithms will make a big difference is healthcare.[17] The keeping and administration of medical files is increasingly being automated to provide an interconnected and fast delivery of information to doctors.[18] Transforming the healthcare industry will also impact medical research, hence better results can be achieved in saving human lives.[19] Doctors making use of technology to detect disease and subsequently propose treatment will become more accurate and truly evidence-based. For example, examining how to increase cancer detection in the images of lymph node cells research showed that an AI-exclusive approach had a 7.5% error rate and a human one a 3.5% error rate. The combined approach, however, revealed an error rate of only 0.5% (85% reduction in error).[20]

Us versus them?

Putting all these developments together makes it clear that the basic cognitive skills and physical abilities that humans have always brought to the table are about to become a thing of the past. These abilities are vulnerable to becoming automated and optimized further by fast-processing, learning machines. It is this vision – widely advocated in the popular press – that makes many of us wonder where the limits of automation lie; if there are any. After all, if even the skills and abilities that are essential to what makes us human seem ready to be replaced by AI, and this new technology is able to engage in deep learning and thus continuously improve, what will be left for humans in the future?

This reflection is not a new one. In fact, it has been around for quite some time. Indeed, in 1965 British mathematician I.J. Good wrote, "An ultra-intelligent machine could design even better machines; there would then unquestionably be an 'intelligence explosion,' and the intelligence of man would be left far behind." In all fairness, such speculation introduces several existential questions. And, it is those kinds of questions that make people very nervous today about the future of humanity in an ecosystem where technology that may overtake us has arrived. In fact, it introduces us to a potential conflict of interest that will make it hard for us to choose.

On one hand, we are clearly obsessed with the power of AI to bring many benefits to our organizations and society. On the other hand, however, this obsession also creates a moment of reflection that worries us. A reflection that confronts us with the realization that human limits can be solved by technology; ultimately, this means that applying technology may render humans obsolete. In our pursuit for more profit and growth, and a desire to increase efficiency, we may be confronted with a sense of disappointment about what it actually means to be human.

This kind of reflective and critical thinking about humanity makes clear that although we fear being replaced, we do look at *humans* and *machines* as two different entities. We make a big distinction between humans as *us* and machines as *them*. Because of this sentiment, it is clear that the idea of *we* (humans and machines together) may be difficult to accept. So, if this is the case, how on earth can we talk about a partnership between humans and machines? If we think we are so different that becoming one is impossible, coexistence will be the best situation possible. But even coexistence is feared by many, because this may still lead to humans being replaced by the superior machine.

All these concerns point out that we consider humans as actors that are limited in their abilities, whereas we regard machines as entities that can develop and reach heights that ultimately humans will be unable to reach. But, is this a *valid* assumption? What does science say? Much of the research out there seems to provide evidence that this view may indeed be valid. Studies do suggest that if we look at how people judge the potential of new technology, approach its functionality and predict how to use it in the future, the conclusion seems to be that humans fear being outperformed. Why does science suggest such a conclusion?

Since the 1970s, scholars have been providing evidence that human experts do not perform as well as simple linear models in things like clinical diagnosis, forecasting graduate students' success, and other prediction tasks.[21,22] Findings like this have led to the idea that algorithmic judgment is superior to expert human judgment.[23] For example, research has shown that algorithms deliver more accurate medical diagnoses when detecting heart-rate diseases.[24,25,26]

Furthermore, in the world of business, algorithms prove better at predicting employee performance, the products customers want to buy, and identifying fake news and information.[27,28] An overall analysis of all these effects (what is called a meta-analysis) even reveals that algorithms outperform human forecasters by 10% on average.[29] Overall, the evidence suggests that it is (and will increasingly be) the case that algorithms outperform humans.

This scientific evidence, combined with our tendency to think of humans and machines as us versus them, poses the question of whether

AI will replace people's jobs at center-stage.[30] This question is no longer a peripheral one. It dominates many discussions in business and society, to the extent that websites now exist where one can discover the likelihood of your job being automated in the next 20 years.

In fact, we do not even have to wait for this scenario to happen. For example, in 2018 online retailer Shop Direct announced the closure of warehouses because nearly 2,000 jobs had become automated. The largest software company in Europe, SAP, has also eliminated several thousands of jobs by introducing AI into their management structure.

The framework for today's society is clearly dominated by the assumption that humans will be replaced by technology whenever possible (human-out-of-the-loop) and that it only makes sense for humans to be part of the business process when automation is not yet possible (contingent participation). Several surveys indicate that it is only a matter of time. For example, an Accenture study revealed that 85% of surveyed executives want to invest more extensively in AI-related technologies by 2020.[31] Likewise, a PwC survey revealed that 62% of executives are planning to deploy AI in several management areas.[32] Furthermore, a survey by Salesforce Research revealed that, in the service industry, 69% of organizations are actively preparing for AI-based service solutions to be applied. Finally, Yahoo Finance predicts that in 2040 our workforce "may be totally unrecognizable."[33]

Why we think about replacing humans

Where does this obsession with replacing humans come from? Is it the human default that once we find a limitation – in this case, our own – we believe it must be eliminated and replaced? Is there simply no room for the weak? A matter of accepting that once a stronger villain arrives in town, the old (and weaker) one is replaced? If this is the case, then this kind of thinking will transform the discussion about the human-AI relationship into a zero-sum game. If one is better (and thus wins), then the other loses (and is eliminated). Where does the belief in this logic come from?

To answer this question, it is worthwhile to look at the distinction that the famous French philosopher René Descartes made between mind and body.[34] The body allowed us to do physical work, but, with the industrial revolution taking place, we were able to replicate our physical strength by utilizing machines. The enormous advantage was that we could now work faster and create more growth and profit. Importantly, however, it also allowed us to free ourselves from physical labor and move our attention towards the power of our brain. This led to humans becoming more sophisticated and creative, and able to come up with new ways of dealing with reality. Our move towards the mind, and away from the body, meant that we submitted for the first time to the machine. With machines doing the mindless physical work, rendering the human body obsolete, we were then able to devote most of our time to work that requires the application of the mind.

In the 21st century, it is our mind that is now being challenged by the technology revolution. Our mental capacity simply cannot compete with the speed of algorithms to process data, as well as their ability to learn and optimize any outcome in almost unlimited ways. These developments mean that, as a society, we have entered yet another phase of great opportunities which can benefit and further our interests. However, the opportunity available is not the augmentation of our physical strength to bring material success, but the augmentation of our cognitive strength. When using the idea of the body and mind to look at these developments, we may well have reason to be afraid.

In the past, we became dependent on the machine to do our physical work. If the present and future follows the path of the past, does this mean that we will now also become dependent on technology to do the work of the mind? If we adopt a rational point of view, where we consider ourselves as primarily striving for optimization, this kind of dependence will definitely happen. We know that we live in a time where a new type of *super* mind – AI that goes well beyond the cognitive abilities of humans – has arrived. At the same time, we are being bombarded with news that the authentic human sense of intelligence is failing when we compare it to the efficiencies of artificial intelligence.

Obviously, it is somewhat of an irony that we have created this challenge ourselves. Beyond that, it is a cynical sentiment that reminds us the end may be near. In fact, if algorithms now replace the human mind (after the machine replaced the body), we may have nowhere else to run. Wasn't it the case that there is only body and mind? If both are replaced, in which direction do humans move? Do we need to now think about whether the human race is needed at all? Is it time to ask ourselves where, if at all, we can use humans in the cycle of algorithms that we are creating?

As indicated earlier, for some jobs (e.g. financial industry, health care) automation seems to be rapidly becoming the dominant voice. But, towards the future, it will not only be in those industries where humans will become inferior to algorithms. Telling in this respect is the 2018 Deloitte Global Human Capital Trends survey and report of business and HR leaders. This survey found that 72% of leaders indicated that AI, robots, and automation are quickly becoming the most important investment areas.

When innovating becomes leading

If body and mind can be replaced, man itself should be replaced. It sounds like science fiction, but all the signs seem to be there. So, if this is really happening, the question of whether we submit to the machine and corresponding technology will be the next one to answer.

In the volatile and uncertain business environment of today, this idea may not sound too crazy. Hasn't it been suggested that the kind of leader needed to survive such circumstances is one who has superior data management and utilization skills? One who is able to produce specific cost-saving recommendations, and enables organizational efficiency and productivity? And, most importantly, is able to deliver all of this at lightning speed! Yes, from this point of view, ladies and gentlemen, we could argue that the demand for a new leader has arrived and it is not the human kind. In fact, as a society we have landed in a new industrial revolution – and this one is led by algorithms. Human leadership may not even survive the impact of AI. If so, will this change of leadership happen smoothly and without opposition?

Given all the benefits that our new automated leader brings us, resistance may not only be futile, but even non-existent. It should be, if we as humans react rationally. As rational beings we should strive for maximizing our own interests. And, as we can see it now, all the benefits coming along with the increase of automation can only create more efficient lives for us. So, our rationality says a big *yes* to this new leadership situation.

But it is not only our rationality that is at play. Emotions are likely to play a role as well. All the benefits also create a comfortable situation that humans will easily adjust to and may even become addicted to. And, once we become addicted to it, we will comply with it because it makes us happy. As a matter of fact, research shows that machines can trigger the reward centers in our brain (one of the reasons why humans have become so addicted to continuously checking their smartphones). The reward center releases the hormone dopamine, which creates a feeling of happiness. But, as with any addiction, humans will run the risk of looking for these rewards more often. They want to maintain this feeling of happiness, so they will increasingly feel a need for more automation. Since our automated leader seems to be able to give us what we want, and as such make us addicted, human compliance is likely to follow. OK, it is clear humans will surrender. Autonomous algorithms are here to stay and – could it really be true? – will lead us.

But, before you close this book and accept the idea of an algorithm telling you tomorrow what to do, might I introduce you to another reality? A reality that brings a more complex view on leadership and the potential role that algorithms will play. Allow me to start with a first request. Think about the question of whether an optimizing leader really constitutes leadership? Is a leader simply the combination of being a strong and smart person? Is leadership something that can be achieved by the body and mind combined into one role? If so, then the smart machine of today is truly the winner. But, I do beg to differ. For the sake of the argument, let us take a quick look at how exactly algorithms learn and whether this fits the leadership process as we know it in today's (human) society.

Do limits exist for self-learning machines?

To understand how algorithms learn, it is necessary to introduce the English mathematician Alan Turing. Depicted by actor Benedict Cumberbatch in the movie *The Imitation Game*, Alan Turing is best known for his accomplishment of deciphering the Enigma code used by the Germans during the second world war. To achieve this, he developed an electro-mechanical computer, which was called the Bombe. The fact that the Bombe achieved something that no human was capable of led Turing to think about the intelligence of the machine.

This led to his 1950 article, 'Computing Machinery and Intelligence,' in which he introduced the now-famous Alan Turing test, which is today still considered the crucial test to determine whether a machine is truly intelligent. In the test, a human interacts with another human and a machine. The participant cannot see the other human or the machine and can only use information on how the other unseen party behaves. If the human is not able to distinguish between the behavior of another human and the behavior of a machine, it follows that we can call the machine intelligent. It is these behavioral ideas of Alan Turing that are today still significantly influencing the development of learning algorithms.

The fact that observable behaviors form the input to learning is not a surprise as in the time of Turing behavioral science was dominating. This stream within psychology refrained from looking inside the mind of humans. The mind was considered the black box of humans (interestingly enough the same is being said of AI nowadays), as it was not directly observable. For that reason, scientists back then suggested that the mind should not be studied. Only behaviors could be considered the true indicators of what humans felt and thought.

To illustrate the dominance of this way of thinking, consider the following joke: Two behaviorists walk into a bar. One says to the other: "You're fine. How am I?" In a similar vein, today we assume that algorithms can learn by analysing data in ways that identify observable patterns. And those patterns teach algorithms the rules of the game. Based on these rules they make inferences and construct models that guide predictions. Thus, in a way, we could say that algorithms decide and advise strategies based on the patterns observed in data. These patterns inform the algorithm what the common behavior is (the rule of the context of the data) and subsequently the algorithm adjusts to it.

Algorithms thus act in line with the data holding observable patterns with which they are being fed. These observable patterns (which reflect the behaviors Turing referred to), however, do not lead algorithms to learn what lies behind these patterns. Or, in other words, they do not allow algorithms to understand the feelings and deeper level of thinking, reflection and pondering that hide beneath the observable behaviors. This reality means that algorithms can perfectly imitate (hence, the title of the movie) and pretend to be human, but can they really be human in being able to function in relationships in the manner of leaders? Can algorithms, which supposedly display human (learned) behaviors, really survive and function in human social relationships?

Consider the following example. Google Duplex recently demonstrated AI having a flawless conversation over the phone when making an appointment for a dinner.[35] The restaurant owner did not have a clue he was talking to AI making the reservation. But imagine what would happen if unexpected events occurred during such a conversation? (Note, the mere fact that you are able to imagine such a scenario makes you already different from the algorithm who would never consider this scenario.) What if the restaurant owner suddenly had a change of heart and told AI that he does not want to work that evening, despite the fact that it is mentioned online that the restaurant will be open that same evening? Will AI be able to take perspective and give a reasonable (human) response?

In all honesty, this may be less likely. It is one thing for an algorithm to know the behaviors that humans usually show and based on those observations develop a behavioral repertoire to deal with most situations. It is, however, another thing to understand the meaning behind human behaviors and respond to it in an equally meaningful way. And here lies the potential limitation for the algorithm as a leader. At this moment, an algorithm cannot understand the meaning of behavior in a given context. AI learns and operates in a context-free way, whereas humans have the ability to account for the situation when behaviors are shown – and, importantly, we expect this skill from leaders. It is as Melanie Mitchell noted in her book *Artificial Intelligence: A Guide for Thinking Humans*: "Even today's most capable AI systems have crucial limitations. They are good only at narrowly defined tasks and utterly clueless about the world beyond."

As a side note, this logic of meaning and taking perspective is something that unfortunately seems to be forgotten by those saying that we have replaced Descartes's body and mind, making humans less needed. Yes, Descartes identified the two separate entities of body and mind, but he also noted that they are connected. We still use this assumption today when we say a healthy mind makes for a healthy body. But what makes for the connection? What is the glue that holds mind and body so closely aligned? In philosophical terms we may say it is the soul. The soul that gives us passion, emotions and a sense of intuitive interpretation with respect to the things we see, do and decide. As such, we may be able to replace the body and the mind, but do the ones replacing us also have the soul to make the total entity work? If body and mind cannot connect, then leadership without heart is the consequence.

And, think about it, would you then simply comply and follow orders from an intelligent machine leader? Those who are big fans of the Star Trek movies will know the character Data. Data is a humanoid robot who is trying to learn how to understand human emotion. In one episode, Data has to take over the command of the Starship USS Enterprise. This experience turned out to be a useful lesson for both the robot and the human crew for how important human emotions are to leadership.

Today, we have arrived in an era where this scenario may not be science fiction for too much longer. But with such futuristic views on leadership in sight, we also need to understand the kind of society and organizations we would like to see. How do we want to lead them? We need to come up with an answer to what leadership means to us and who should take up the leadership position, including assessing our own strengths and weaknesses.

CHAPTER 2

The Leadership Challenge in the Algorithm Age

T HE MACHINE AGE arrived a long time ago, but today's need for the machine seems to know no limits. Modern machines need more room, more execution power and yes, maybe also the desire to lead. But who will they lead? The answer is, those who need the machine the most. And, dear reader, this may well turn out to be humans.

Naqvi writes that "the need of the machine could not be fulfilled without getting the followers to co-operate."[36] As we will see later, the influence that leaders achieve – and which we will call the process of leadership – can only be accomplished if there are others out there willing to follow the directives, ideas and suggestions of the one leading. So, if machines are about to become leaders, they need followers to achieve the powers and potential that we attribute to those same machines. As humans have developed an obsession to ensure optimal use of the potential attributed to machines, it follows that the followers are likely to be those same humans. It is a string of thought that keep the minds of scholars today very occupied.

Of course, many among us may wonder whether a machine (empowered by the workings of algorithms) leading the human species is actually a valid proposition. Why should we even reflect on the possibility of algorithms leading organizations populated by humans? Does it make sense to ponder whether your next boss will be an algorithm? What should we do about it? Does 'Leadership by Algorithm' even have a basis to exist? And, if so, do we really need it?

To delve deeper into this series of questions, we first need to ask ourselves whether it is a reasonable thing to expect human employees to follow algorithm-driven leaders in the same way they would a human leader? Can such a world exist? Some scholars think so.

These scholars assume that whoever becomes the leader is determined, to a large extent, by the situation at hand. One of the most prominent leadership scholars, Jeffrey Pfeffer, supported this view in his 1977 *Academy of Management Review* piece, 'The Ambiguity of Leadership'. In his article, Pfeffer debunks the myth that leaders are a unique kind of species – independent of any situational influence. Pfeffer argues that in our human drive to see heroes as the true leaders, we adopt the illusion that only those individuals who bring something special to the table can be called leaders. (As a side note, when looking at the contemporary movie industry, with its focus on the Avengers franchise and other action heroes, it is clear that today we still have a need for the illusion of grand and heroic leadership.)

But, interestingly enough, it is actually the other way around; the situation makes the leader. And history supports this, revealing examples where leadership is attributed to those who, for reasons other than their own unique capabilities, win wars (Sun Tzu's *The Art of War*), or can give the impression that their office is doing wonders for the economy (President Donald Trump bragging that ten years without recession is his own doing).

One of the most extreme examples of this in my lifetime is President George W. Bush and the tragedy of 9/11. Before the Twin Towers and the Pentagon were hit by hijacked airplanes, Bush had some of the lowest leadership ratings since records began. In the aftermath of these events, he visited Ground Zero and announced that the US would punish those responsible. And something extraordinary happened. Suddenly, a man considered by most as incapable of taking on the role of President of the United States was elevated to one of the highest ratings for leadership ever recorded. The situation caused Bush to be seen by many as a good leader, especially when he expressed aggression and optimism, and took the actions of a leader going to war.

The power of the situation to decide who will lead has been proven by various scientific studies of mayors, athletic coaches and corporate leaders.[37,38] These insights have led to the conclusion that if the situational demands dictate leadership effectiveness in the eyes of others, then "what does it matter who occupies the position or how they behave?"[39]

Will your boss be a robot?

These acclaimed insights seem to suggest that it is OK for algorithms to take up the role of leader. Just as it is OK for humans to take on this role. So, if this is true, why worry about automated leadership?

If it does not matter, then, as humans, we should take even more responsibility to ask whether algorithms are really able to lead organizations. Today's organizations are faced with a volatile business environment and are therefore required to act in fast and agile ways. To meet these demands, humans seek to explore how technology can help us to operate more efficiently and manage optimal performance. For instance, technological innovation is needed to ensure that our organizations can adapt to deliver products and services to a market populated with demanding customers. There is no way to escape this truth. It is the situation that we are faced with!

Our business environment demands algorithms to be part of promoting organizational efficiency. Knowing the power of situational influences, it may not seem such a crazy idea at all that those running our organizations in the pursuit to excel may well become dictated by algorithms. Or, in other words, algorithms may well drive the management process very soon.

This is not simply a thought exercise anymore. Being confronted with greater expectations of productivity, the need to respond faster, and the requirement to be more rational and data driven in our responses, both business and thought leaders have put the idea to automate leadership firmly on the table. Few are now questioning if this is feasible, instead they are wondering how best to implement their AI management strategy. Business leaders have embraced the idea that the widely announced digital disruption has introduced many challenges. Maybe too many for humans to deal with. As a result, it has made the business world uncertain on how to manage digital disruption. If this is the case, should it then not be better to rewrite the leadership handbooks that we have written over the last few decades?

Our organizations have become so complex that running them seems to require a leader with almost superhuman abilities. The world moves too fast for human leaders to be confident that they will make good decisions. Even though human intelligence may be a beautiful and complex thing, the simple reality is that it is not always up to the job of processing massive amounts of data, in very short periods of time, to arrive at the best decision available. And, this is where the algorithm jumps into the leadership equation. Algorithms can replace almost any feature that we think of as representing good leadership. We have arrived at a time where, "for any given skill one can think of, some computer scientists may already be trying to develop an algorithm to do it".[40] As a result, it is not a utopian idea any more to point out that the future management of organizations will be an automated one.[41] It will prove to be cheaper, more efficient, and potentially more impartial in its actions than human beings.

I would even go further: Given the market demand for business efficiency, it is inevitable that algorithms are and will be replacing various jobs at different levels of managerial discretion and as such seem destined to take over leadership from humans in many ways.[42] As Frank Pasquale noted, "authority is increasingly expressed algorithmically".[43] In fact, having algorithms as part of how authority looks and sounds, moves the algorithm by definition into the role of power holder. How so? Think about it, because of their deep learning abilities, algorithms construct decision rules that are not well understood by humans. Their decisions will therefore feel fixed and in some way intractable. If we thus allow algorithms to take up the role of the authority, we will become dependent on them. In other words, if we voluntarily make algorithms part of our leadership system, then we create a context where we will be dependent on them. In addition, this dependency will – because of the rational nature of an algorithm – feel distant, rigid and hard to argue with. The result will be that algorithms will co-ordinate what we do and how we do it.

The red-hot business model

If algorithms have the power to shape our interactions, how does the corporate world factor this into their ideas on how to run a company? Well, it seems increasingly likely that they are embracing a new business model, where algorithms lead in the management of decisions and execution of jobs, and human employees follow.[44] For example, the analytics provider SAS considers digital data management as a step forward, where algorithms not only provide advice but also fuel strategic decision-making.[45] This business model portrays human employee's bosses as the smart ones, since they are driven by algorithms that can perform in superior ways. No doubt this business model is clearly present in the minds of many as it drives important leadership transformations currently taking place in organizations.

Efforts are underway to understand the brains of successful CEOs and use those neural imprints to create highly efficient algorithms.[46] These algorithms will continuously learn and develop into a leading authority, superior even to human leaders. Results from a survey conducted by the World Economic Forum's Global Agenda Council on the Future of Software and Society also revealed that businesspeople expect artificially intelligent machines to be part of a company's board of directors by 2026. As a matter of fact, this futuristic view is already materializing. For example, the Hong-Kong based venture-capital firm Deep Knowledge recently appointed a decision-making algorithm – known as VITAL – to its board of directors, indicating that algorithms are already taking on the leadership challenge to set parameters of corporate governance.[47,48] And, last, but not least, in 2019, Amazon allowed AI to fire employees without consulting with any human.[49]

It is important to realize, however, that there is also the potential for all of these optimistic and exciting developments to backfire. They could create a situation where people are increasingly being confronted with existential doubts and fears about their vision of the future. Indeed, although algorithms bring economic benefits, people may feel that human labor is devalued by organizations aggressively pursuing automation.[50] As a result, the value of being a human employee is not understood very well anymore and the fear for unemployment is a real one.

In addition, existential doubts may create the need to reflect on what kind of society we want to see. Do we want a society where the corporate dream of having optimally functioning organizations leads us towards automation of those leading us? Or do we want a society where we decide not to forego the human touch in whatever we do, including leadership?

Such feelings cannot be underestimated because they directly link to many people's uncertainties about whether their job will still be relevant in the new technology era. Many also question what the future of human employees will be if algorithms run the decision-making process. It is these uncertainties that I, as a business school professor, am faced with when executives ask whether leadership courses, which provide insight into human motivation, will disappear in the future. This is the point where I see it is necessary to disrupt our thinking about the business models we want to adapt and the kind of automated leaders we want to see in the future.

It is all well and good to have these models in mind. Its exciting, even, to see where the limits of those models may lie in our pursuit to optimize performance, organizations and society. However, it is also the responsibility of humans to be critical about their own ambitions, desires and wildest dreams. Because, what one can imagine is not necessarily what we need, nor is it necessarily the vision that is driven by the best and most accurate information. In fact, alongside all the exciting technological developments that we witness today, when it comes down to automating our business leadership, we need to realize that those wishes could well be driven by people who are poorly informed about the real impact of automated work forces.

Human sophistication

So, the evolving business model of the future seems to be one designed and pushed by people who do not necessarily have the required knowledge of what algorithms are capable of, nor of what kind of human skills are necessary to drive leadership excellence.

It is a fact that many business leaders cannot be recognized as experts in technology, its applications and usage, and philosophical thought regarding the human reality that develops in an automated environment. So, despite all the greatness and beauty behind the idea that increasing automation will inevitably lead to automation of everything, including the leadership of organizations, we also have to be critical about what exactly has real value and what has not. In this respect, it is interesting that, contrary to the preferred automation model of business leaders, recent research has revealed that skills related to feelings will define the future jobs for humans. In fact, salaries for human employees in the future are expected to be determined more by the ability to deal with emotions and relationships rather than by their cognitive abilities. This reality paints a future where jobs that require sensitivity to needs for relationships will have to be populated by humans and the role of leadership seems to fit that bill.

The argument that I am putting forward is that the functioning of our organizations and societies are not served by a kind of sentiment that the analysis of data by algorithms will automatically develop and lead strategies in miraculous ways. Algorithms are not technological tools that have the leading abilities to deliver immediate returns without any human presence or interference needed. As we see technology develop today, we need to be aware of the fact that automated decision-making is still something of a black-box that runs in less structured ways than we think. Algorithms also miss human sophistication, and an awareness of moral norms and emotions; all skills that allow leaders to create value beyond the immediate observable financial returns. In fact, when looking at the data available, reality paints a somewhat different vision when it comes down to the optimal use of algorithms in leading and co-ordinating organizations.

Research by IBM shows that 41% of CEOs report that their organization is not at all prepared to introduce data analytic tools into their management structures.[51] In addition, when it comes down to dealing with humans in automated ways, only about 22% of organizations say that they have adopted algorithms in their Human Resources practices.[52] And, of those 22%, most are not clear on what the exact effect is that the algorithms reveal. Given these numbers, it seems reasonable to argue that wise leadership in the 21st century will still need more of a strategy than simply trying to make a difference by means of optimizing the technology (including the management technology) taking care of our data. Rather the real difference will be made in having leadership out there that can make use of these technologies in human-centred and sustainable ways that benefit human values, interests and well-being.

CHAPTER 3

Leading by Algorithm: Rushing In

R ECOGNIZED AS THE new big thing, algorithms are ready to penetrate many of our daily activities and tasks. The reality, however, is that algorithms are not just preparing to dominate our lives, they *already do*.

Algorithms drive machines by telling them what to do to in order to produce what humans want to see. Yes, algorithms are not only the eagerly awaited, super intelligent aspect of the AI hype, but also the driver of ubiquitous machines we use today in a routine way, such as computers. Algorithms are thus already a pivotal part of our society, and their level of influence is only expected to increase over time.

I am emphasizing this omnipresence of algorithms today and in the future since many people in reality have no clear idea of *what* algorithms are and, as such, miss out on how we should assess the real value and application of algorithms in our work settings. This is an important observation to note because businesses seem happy to embrace the idea that leadership by algorithm will be the next evolutionary step to take. And if we plan to delegate the influence that leaders have over others to an algorithm, then we also need to understand *who* these leaders are.

If we think about leadership, we quickly arrive at specific types of individuals with specific skills, or, in other words, we have clear expectations and views on the identity of the people we consider to be leaders. Because we have those expectations, humans are able to quickly decide what kind of leader we need when situations change. Or, to put it differently, human psychology works in such a way that when a situation with specific demands presents itself, we can quickly infer the kind of leader that is needed. Given these situational demands, we will easily accept a leader with certain skills as the one in charge and comply with their directives.

Business today is confronted with much uncertainty, a volatile market, and rapid changes requiring leadership that is able to deal with complex and ever-changing situations. Algorithms and their unique capabilities of being rational and consistent in dealing with complex and highly ambiguous events seem to fit the bill to lead in such business situations. In fact, as I have documented earlier, today's changing business environment is making the algorithm a prime candidate for tomorrow's leader.

But is this really true? Can we make such a decision based on our perceived understanding of what the situation demands and the abilities an algorithm presents? Especially if we are not even clear how the algorithm is to be defined within the context of our society?

When it comes down to putting algorithms on the world stage as leaders-to-be, we need to become better informed about the real leadership potential that this new technology has before we blindly commit to automation. For effective leadership to emerge, one necessary condition is that any future leader is able to offer an identity that can be trusted. It is the presence of trust that makes people voluntarily engage in an open and co-operative relationship with the leader. It is only when relationships are characterized by open-mindedness and collaborative behavior that the influence of an effective leader can kick in. Put simply, if the actor placed in the leader role is not trusted, no leadership can emerge.

Being wise, not smart

So, how do algorithms fare in this respect? The late Peter Drucker once noted that "the computer makes no decisions; it only carries out orders. It's a total moron, and therein lies its strength. It forces us to think, to set the criteria. The stupider the tool, the brighter the master has to be – and this is the dumbest tool we have ever had."[53]

If Peter Drucker's wisdom proves still to be true today, then we need to worry, because a potential leadership disaster may be circling above our heads. If algorithms move into a leadership role and fulfil the tasks dealing with a rapidly changing world, then a problem is likely to occur. That problem will center around whether or not algorithms do possess the skills to acquire influence to lead others. After all, leaders today need to be influential as they have to develop truly global organizations that operate effortlessly across borders. To achieve such influence, scholars have argued that a sense of wise leadership is needed.[54] Are algorithms capable of doing so? If they are not, then we may have made algorithms appear to be wiser than they really are. And if this is the case, we need to be more careful in our assessment of how and when algorithms can be used in matters of authority.

Building on this logic, an important question to address is whether algorithms can really be wise while not being human? Again, research can help here. What we know so far, is that studies have shown that people perceive machines in general, and algorithms more specifically, as non-human. We perceive them this way for the simple reason that we are unable to attribute a "complete mind" to a machine.[55] We do not consider machines and algorithms to possess the fully-fledged emotional (experiential) and thinking (agency) capabilities of humans. You may ask yourself whether it is necessary that machines need to possess the entire range of human emotions and cognitions for them to assume the role of leaders. Well, understanding that people only follow leaders if they perceive them to be legitimate, and that legitimacy is inferred from our perceptions of whether someone is wise, fair and mindful, then it is indeed necessary.

Research in psychology shows that – as humans – we only consider someone or something to have a mind when we can attribute both agency and experience to them.[56] As algorithms are perceived to be limited in their abilities to show empathy or even understand the true meaning of human emotions, we look at them as not having a complete mind. Furthermore, if we consider someone else not to have a complete mind, and the ability to recognize and understand emotions, it is safe to assume that we also do not want this other one to make ethical choices on our behalf. If this is the case, then this consequence of not being able to make ethical choices obviously complicates the idea of algorithms taking up any leadership position. Leaders are expected to serve our interests and make the appropriate decisions to do so.

So, this should be the end of the story and algorithms should simply not move into leadership roles.

Right?

The leadership of today will not be the leadership of tomorrow

Maybe it is not the end of the story, but rather a new beginning. If we listen to popular media, business press and visionary keynotes, algorithms may still be in the leadership game – maybe even more than ever. Indeed, despite science identifying several important limitations that impede algorithms from taking up decision-making responsibilities, this has not prevented discussion on whether leadership by algorithm should still occur. The idea that algorithms can run organizations is not one that is dead and buried, but rather alive and kicking.

How then can this discussion about automated leadership survive and even be envisioned as the future leadership model? One possible reason may be that this leadership-by-algorithm *hype* in essence indicates a frustration with today's (human) leadership. As a result, business and society at large may be looking for different forms of leadership. So, it seems likely that we are looking for a different kind of wisdom in our leaders of tomorrow. And, that kind of new wisdom could well be provided by an algorithm.

What I am saying is that we may have entered an era where we do not consider it necessary for our future business leaders to possess the kind of wisdom that we so dearly attribute to humans. Rather, it may be that we define the wisdom for our future leaders in terms of other attributes and skills. It could well be that we are looking for a kind of leadership that is best equipped to provide the most accurate and, at the same time, fastest decisions. If we want those decision-making qualities to be reflected in our future leaders, then it should not be a surprise that we are ready to embrace the idea of leadership by algorithm. After all, isn't it the case that leaders able to make fast and accurate decisions should also be able to best manage a volatile business environment?

Interestingly, when we look at leadership literature, scholars in the past have portrayed good leadership as those who "make good decisions in a timely way."[57] We know that leaders have to make decisions on a daily basis. We also know that those decisions reveal important social consequences that can benefit or harm the organization and its employees.[58,59] For these reasons, today's focus in the digital era may be more on selecting leaders who are able to deal with data in the most optimal way. And, subsequently, we recognize suddenly the beauty of an algorithm as a likely candidate to make decisions and, hence, lead.

If we move from our theoretical exercise above and on to what we see in practice, we may find some evidence in favour of leadership by algorithm. The one thing that is not going unnoticed is that jobs are increasingly being automated, with algorithms integrated into decision-making processes. This trend could be interpreted as a signal that a new kind of automated leadership may well be on its way.

And, why should this be? Well, the faster acting, more accurate and consistent self-learning algorithms become, the more likely it could be that humans will gradually transfer the power to lead to those same algorithms. Today's reality is that companies operate in complex and volatile business environments where a need for faster and more accurate decision-making is increasingly emerging. To be able to deal with this need, people begin to seek a new kind of leader to get the job done. This new kind of leader seems to be recognized as one that is automated, thinks rationally and, hence, offers a sense of accuracy and precision to provide the most optimal choice in any kind of situation.

Are we ready to accept?

At this moment, you may wonder whether our need and desire for this kind of new leader is not simply wishful thinking. On one hand, humans surely would not so easily transfer the power and influence of their leaders to an automated entity. On the other hand, maybe we are too sentimental about these questions. It is this emotional reaction that prevents us from turning leadership as we know it today into a more optimal form that may well be less human.

After all, from a rational point of view, we should do anything possible to optimize our way of doing business. Such efforts, without a doubt, should also include thinking about how we can run our organizations and make decisions in better, more optimized ways. If we are serious about thinking in a rational fashion about how we want to approach the future of work, it should only be a matter of time before automated leadership will happen.

Some research actually suggests that people today are ready to accept this idea. A 2019 study by Logg, Minson and Moore examined the attitude of humans towards the judgments and advice offered by algorithms. They arrived at some powerful conclusions.[60] The authors concluded the following: "Our studies suggest that people are often comfortable accepting guidance from algorithms, and sometimes even trust them more than other people. … It may not be necessary to invest in emphasizing the human element of [the] process. Maybe companies that present themselves as primarily driven by algorithms, like Netflix and Pandora, have the right idea."

These recent studies clearly underscore the idea that humans may not be so sentimental about the *future leadership* question and are actually more willing to trust the input and direction that algorithms provide than we expected. And, importantly, this tendency does not seem to be the case only in the context of experimental studies, but also in real life. We know that Uber riders respond in a more negative way to a price increase if it is set by a human, compared to when it is set by an algorithm. If a human sets out new guidelines that harm the self-interest of other humans, then those others will be less forgiving than when an algorithm initiates this policy.

After all, if a decision made by a human leads to negative consequences for another human, then it is usually evaluated as intentional. Whereas, when an algorithm makes a decision that leads to negative consequences for a human, people do not perceive the algorithm to have acted intentionally. Indeed, as discussed earlier, people do not perceive an algorithm to have a *mind* and therefore it is difficult to see how an algorithm could have bad intentions.

This shows that, under certain circumstances, humans actually prefer algorithms to make choices because they are not considered to be threatening to us. A recent study published in *Nature Human Behaviour* consolidated this idea.[61] Studies revealed that human employees showed a stronger preference for being replaced by an algorithm than by another human. This is quite a surprising finding in light of the current debate that people are fearful of being replaced by AI. But then again, from the point of view that people may be more lenient toward having rationally-acting algorithms to make decisions on their behalf, it may not be that surprising. Researchers in this study found that the reason behind their finding was that humans experienced being replaced by another human to be more harmful to their self-interest. To be more precise, they considered being replaced by another human to be more threatening to their public image (how they are perceived by others) and self-esteem.

In fact, if you are replaced by another human, people may quickly reason that this other person is better than you. This judgment is something people obviously do not like, because it implies that others will have a negative view of you and your abilities (i.e. which is part of your public image). On the other hand, if you – as a human – are being replaced by an algorithm, you are being replaced by a non-human, and this event is experienced as less threatening to your public image. Indeed, a human and non-human are completely different species and therefore cannot be compared in the same dimension.

Both the Uber and research findings in *Nature Human Behaviour* illustrate circumstances where people prefer an algorithm to be in charge, as opposed to a human. Thus, these observations emphasize that humans are more inclined to rely on the actions and advice offered by algorithms exactly because they are non-human and, as such, take out the emotional and biased side of human decision makers. It may well be the case that humans are getting ready to see the benefits of a rationally-acting non-human machine to replace those positions that need more optimal and responsible decision making. Leadership positions, for example.

If our leaders do not let their intentions and biased judgments play a role in the decisions they take, we, as humans, will take it less personally and will be more assured of the decision being fair. From that point of view, we see that algorithms are gaining ground quickly in the area where they can provide advice to customers and act as experts to higher-level managers in organizations. For example, recent surveys among customer support and service operations report up to 85% willingness to use virtual assistants by 2020, leading to expectations that in the near future we will witness a significant increase in chatbot use by companies.[62,63]

Who qualifies?

What to think of all of this? Well, if we take into account the fact that businesses today operate in volatile and complex business environments, and therefore require fast and optimal decisions; the recent scientific evidence; and the optimistic vision of business people that automation will hit all levels of authority, then we can only conclude that leadership by algorithm is the best way forward.

It will happen and apparently for good reason. In fact, online work environments are becoming increasingly popular, and the application of algorithms to monitor, co-ordinate and evaluate performance of employees in these settings is very much present.[64] Even more so, businesses today admit that they are increasingly relying on algorithms to co-ordinate work relationships. Delegating the power of authority to algorithms definitely does not seem like science fiction anymore. But is this really the end of the story? Is the final conclusion that leadership by algorithm will happen and that it will be for the better?

In my view, it is not! Yes, it would be the end of the story if we define leadership in a narrow way. So, what is meant by a *narrow manner*? To answer this question, let us first look at how we are approaching the whole issue of replacing humans with algorithms. Many people, and especially the popular press, only look at the skills that are required to *execute* the job. As we all know, however, doing a job well entails more than simply being able to tick the boxes representing a list of skills. Of course, skills are important and recognized as relatively good predictors of how well employees will perform. But that is not the only thing we need to become influential and effective at work. Another important aspect to ensure effective job execution is that *meaning* is given to the job. For people to stay motivated in their job, it is crucial that their function is understood in the broader organizational setting.

Jobs are part of a broader social context in any organization. And it is because of this broader social context that employees are also required to possess the social skills to talk, negotiate, lobby and collaborate with others. Unfortunately, it is also this element of giving meaning to the job in a broader work environment that is hardly ever a focus in the discussion of whether or not jobs should be automated. I argue that we are facing the same problem when we are talking about whether algorithms should and can move into leadership roles.

In today's discussions, a trend has emerged that leadership is only looked upon as a set of required skills. If all the boxes are ticked, a person should be ready to assume a leadership role. The consequence of looking at the possible automation of leadership in this way is that organizations are too narrow in their thinking about what it takes for automated systems to run the organization. Specifically, this rather narrow way of defining leadership means that organizations will make the simple calculation that if any actor (human or non-human) delivers the skills needed to make decisions in fast and data-driven ways, then they are considered fit to lead. And, looking at the leadership challenge lying ahead of us, algorithms can then be considered very worthy candidates for the leadership job.

Will others follow?

But, let's face it, this is not how leadership works! One key aspect of effective leadership is the influence they exert to motivate, inspire and direct others. Leaders are needed to drive change and for that they need to be able to influence others. A leader can only bring this kind of change, however, if those others are willing to accept and support the decisions taken by the leader.

From your own work experience, it is a given that you expect your leaders to be able to explain why change is needed. We all want our leaders to be able to show what change will look like and what kind of value it can create for us. It is those abilities that can motivate others to follow and, as such, make change happen. Leaders are then considered influential. However, if no one is willing to buy-in to the ideas of change communicated by the leader, then nothing will happen. Under those circumstances, we say that leaders are not influential and unable to change anything!

Why will nothing happen if people do not accept the ideas of a leader? Isn't it the case that someone in a leadership position has the power to make things happen anyway (regardless even of any support)? The simple truth is that as a leader, you need others to get things going.[65] If no one follows, there will be no one to help make change happen. Think about it, how many successful leaders do everything themselves? They don't, because they rely on others to make their vision materialize. So, the key to being an effective leader is to be influential and drive change through those who follow. This process is potentially more important today than ever before.

In today's business environment, leaders have to deal with the challenge of digital disruption. To do this, they are required to bring along a vision and identify the possible directions the organization can take to make this vision happen. To deal with these digital disruptions successfully, simply communicating what needs to be done is not enough – although many business leaders today get stuck in this phase. It is not at the stage of providing direction where the job of being a leader stops. People need to be willing to follow the strategic direction of their leader. So, even if a leader possesses all the technical and analytical skills imaginable, they alone cannot do everything. Leaders need others in the organization (and preferably as many as possible) to take up the challenge of change. Transformation can thus only happen if it is both supported and enacted upon by all within an organization.

The black-box problem

What does this kind of thinking about leadership teach us? It makes clear that if we want to know whether leadership by algorithm is a reality waiting to happen, we need to assess whether this technology is also able to create a culture where employees are willing to be influenced by a leader. So, if an algorithm wants to move into a leadership role, it will need to have the skills to play the influence game as well. And this is where it becomes interesting. If we look at the issue of leadership by algorithm from this point of view, we suddenly see a completely different story emerge. Now, algorithms may not seem to be the best leadership choice after all. Indeed, are algorithms able to touch the heart of human followers and mobilize them to make a vision happen?

To understand whether this is the case, we need to know whether algorithms have the ability to influence humans into adopting an open and trusting attitude towards automated leadership. And, there may be a problem with that. For example, data provided by Davenport reveals that 41.5% of US consumers do not trust AI with their financials and only 4% trusted AI in the employee hiring process.[66]

Giving authority to algorithms is actually seen by many as a frightening future. In 2015, for example, the late Cambridge scholar Stephen Hawking and 3,000 other researchers signed an open letter calling for a ban on autonomous weapons. They felt that algorithms could not be given powers in ways that could threaten our well-being and in a way humanity in its entirety. In fact, most surveys reveal that, at this moment in time, humans feel concerned, suspicious and uncomfortable when dealing with algorithms that make decisions on their behalf.

So, if people are not too optimistic about algorithms being able to motivate humans to be open to their directives, what does science say? An important finding emerging from a large number of studies concerns the general trend that people perceive the functioning of autonomous algorithms as something of a black box. It is this *black-box* perception that leads humans to be suspicious of autonomous algorithms in our work setting.

This suspicion is primarily because information generated by algorithms lack transparency (how was it generated?) and are difficult to explain – even engineers who initially designed the algorithm have struggle to understand its processes.[67,68] So it should be no surprise that human employees hesitate in delegating tasks and execution powers to algorithms. This is because they do not understand what it is that those advanced algorithms do. Such perceptions and associated feelings then also create fertile ground for humans to distrust the employment of algorithms in work settings.[69,70]

With such a state of distrust, we see a situation emerging that makes algorithms obviously less suited to lead. Since algorithms are developed within the safe boundaries of an engineering lab, the reality seems to be that they are simply not equipped to deal with a volatile business environment where social pressures exist. One clear pressure, which introduces additional complexity in the decision-making process, is that employees expect explanations to be given for the decisions that automated systems make. And this social pressure will not decline over time – rather the opposite.

Take, for example, the requirement of the European Union (since summer 2018) that organizations need to be able to communicate in transparent ways on how the employment of their algorithms work; such a measure is increasingly proving problematic.

Trusting algorithms

Does this sense of distrust towards algorithms develop, or is it something that pre-exists in the human mind? If it is the latter, then distrust towards algorithms cannot be avoided. In fact, it will be the default position we have to work around in an increasingly automated world. Research reveals findings consistent with the idea that humans are negatively biased towards the ability of algorithms to make predictions and decisions, which induces distrust. For example, scholars identified biases responsible for the fact that people have a strong preference for forecasts made by humans, weigh human input as more important than algorithmic input, and judge professionals who seek out advice from an algorithm more harshly than when advice is asked of another human.[71,72,73,74] The tendency to avoid using advice from algorithms has been named *algorithm aversion*.[75]

This phenomenon of algorithm aversion can be explained by our earlier observation that humans have a deep sense of distrust towards the use of algorithms and especially so in matters that are important to the interest of humans. In my view, the reason for this distrust as a default attitude towards humans is that a human touch is missing. In other words, even though algorithms can be very accurate and focused on identifying the most optimal decision available, it becomes a different issue when algorithms are making decisions on our behalf. And, this is exactly what leaders do, they make decisions on behalf of others. As such, the challenge introduced is one where we do not doubt the rational and optimizing abilities of algorithms, but rather we do not trust a non-human entity to make decisions that have implications for the interests of humans. Even though we feel that this new technology gives much, nevertheless "humanity is taken away."[76]

As I see it, we have two important pieces of knowledge. Today, we know that algorithms are already champions at doing one thing very well. They may even outperform any human in that specific task or area.[77] However, at the same time, we also know that leading an organization represents a more complex reality; a reality where any decision taken has implications for different human stakeholders. From that point of view, we, as humans, need decision makers to be closely aligned with the notion of humanity.

These two pieces of knowledge bring forward two contradictory views of the prospects for leadership by algorithm. On the one hand, algorithms possess superior skills when it comes to dealing with complex data, and are therefore able to identify trends and possibilities that can optimize our future decisions and strategies. For those who consider leadership as a way to make the most validated and accurate choice for others to follow, this may be music to their ears.

Leadership, however, entails more than just being able to identify accurate judgments and optimize decision making. First of all, even though algorithms can identify new and original ways of looking at challenges, this knowledge still needs to be interpreted in light of the values and goals a leader wishes to achieve. In other words, the output of any algorithm still requires a form of interpretation before deciding what needs to be done – a human touch is certainly needed at this point. Second, leaders need to decide how to motivate people and allow them opportunities to serve their own interests while working for the collective. It seems clear that algorithms may fall short in providing content and guidance in these two areas.

So, where are we now in the discussion on whether leadership by algorithm is a possibility?

The idea that emerges is that both camps clearly differ in their existential views and perspectives on what leaders need to do and what kind of meaning they should create. Such differences may be very difficult to solve (if, indeed, it can be solved). I would argue, however, that we need to look at the question of leadership by algorithm in a different way. We should focus on exploring a condition that can allow us to use algorithms in organizations in the most optimal way, while at the same time keeping the human component of leadership alive to its fullest extent.

As I will discuss in the remainder of this book, the guidance of our organizations is in human hands, but takes place at two different levels of authority. The first type of authority is what we call *managerial* influence. That is, the person in the role of manager. The second type of authority concerns *leadership* influence. This kind of influence refers to the person taking up the role of a leader. Both notions of management and leadership are different in terms of their primary function and how they execute their responsibilities. It is in their functional value that – in my view – lies the solution to understanding the extent to which algorithms can and will be part of the influence process of authorities.

CHAPTER 4
Management Controls, Leadership Conquers

I T IS A common mistake in the business world to use the concepts of management and leadership interchangeably. However, although the roles may appear the same, they could not be further apart when it comes to their exact functions.[78] Understanding the difference between these two concepts and what we use them for is crucial if we want to find out where the most successful applications of algorithms lie in our work context.

Indeed, management and leadership are included in the hierarchical structure of any company, yet their responsibilities and mindset greatly differ. As a result, they influence how employees think, act and feel in different ways. As algorithms are increasingly integrated into our work setting, they will also become part of organizational hierarchies. If this happens, how will management versus leadership be affected?

The art of running an organization

How are organizations being run today? It won't have escaped anyone's attention that most organizations have created a culture that is quite bureaucratic in nature. Boxes need to be ticked, comprehensive matrix systems are used, and everyone is being managed to ensure procedures are followed and the stability of the system is maintained. The paperwork that comes along with it has only increased over the years.[79] Of course, no one wants to be on a ship where the captain has no control over the vessel, so some commonly agreed procedures and systems are needed. In a similar way, those at the top of the organization want to ensure the company is run in efficient and non-chaotic ways.

But I think many will also agree that with increased bureaucracy, the system seems to be more in charge than the human when it comes to running an organization. In a way, this may not be such a big surprise. Wasn't it Max Weber who, more than a century ago, said that as "bureaucracy develops the more perfectly, the more it is 'dehumanized.'" This observation instills a familiar feeling in many of us: that the art of management is very much present in our organizations.

One could say that management today is – more than ever – the foundation upon which companies are run. In fact, large organizations today bury the average first-level employee under eight or more layers of management. Business guru Gary Hamel, visiting professor at London Business School, has even noted that since 1983, the number of managers and administrators in US companies has more than doubled. This increase of numbers cannot be found in any other job category.

Hooray for the administrator

Based on these numbers, it is safe to say that management really matters. So, how then did we arrive in a situation where management has been cultivated into an art form? Well, to answer that we need to go back to the Industrial Revolution – remember, the period where machines replaced our body. Around that time, the size of our organizations increased rapidly and the infrastructure became complex. The inherent risk of such rapid growth is, of course, that chaos will enter the organization. So, how to deal with such growth?

During the Industrial Revolution, very little was known about what was needed to ensure that organizations could grow in a structured and co-ordinated manner. Realizing this gap in our knowledge, the field of modern management – as inspired by people like Chester Barnard – was born. The general idea was that managing an organization required an administrative approach. Specifically, the behavior of individual employees needed to be managed by an administrative system. As such, we entered the age where running an organization became an administrative task where the central focus was on controlling and co-ordinating the behaviors of its human employees.

This administrative focus set the stage for the scholar Frederick Taylor, who in 1911 published his book on *The Principles of Scientific Management*. In this work, Taylor emphasized that the priority should be to use systems based on control mechanisms rather than relying on man to make organizations function more effectively. Taylor made these claims based on his productivity experiments, which showed that unobserved workers were inefficient. Hence, ever since then, managing organizations has held the underlying assumption that whenever humans are involved, constant performance monitoring is needed.[80]

The problem with too many managers

The introduction of management as an area of expertise clearly holds important lessons. First, at a little over a century old, management is still a very young field of inquiry. Second, the manager's role is, in essence, still being classified as an administrative job. As a manager, you keep an eye on the company and keep everything running as smoothly and as efficiently as possible. Borrowed from the French word *ménage*, meaning the stable running of a household, management is meant to ensure that everything in the company stays quiet and peaceful, with few disruptions and no unwanted changes. Building on the meaning of the word, management became connected to the idea that it helps organizations to work efficiently, so that its employees can deliver what is being required (KPI), forecasted and assessed.

Management is therefore crucial in bringing order and consistency to the workplace.[81,82] It does so by planning and budgeting, producing standards that are easy to monitor and adopting a narrow purpose that is not too difficult to measure and easy to maintain. As a result, resources should be allocated in planned ways to increase the efficient working of each department and allow us to make forecasts that are more or less accurate and thus very easily manageable.[83,84]

Order and stability are obviously not bad words. There is no problem with having management co-ordinate exchanges and work within and between departments. The problem that seems to have occurred, however, is that management has taken its job a little too seriously. In fact, as the number of bureaucrats indicate, the focus on administration within companies seems to have taken over completely. It seems to have even reached the point that managing the maintenance of peace and stability is the only focus left, simply because the corresponding and ever-increasing bureaucracy has left no room to do anything else!

Today, the major complaint is that people have too much paperwork to do and too many boxes to tick. For those who fear change, this may be good news because the system ensures that there is very little risk that work culture will become disrupted and turn into chaos. For those who are averse to maintaining the status quo, and want to encourage change for the sake of growth, this completely overwhelming administrative approach is nothing short of a nightmare.

Why your mindset matters

Most of you will know that it is not only individuals who see this problem, organizations themselves have also reached this conclusion. Companies across the globe complain that they have too many managers and not enough leaders.

Many companies are saying that while administration costs continue to rise, they can only see a work force that is becoming paralyzed (by the paperwork) and, as a result, no real innovation happens anymore. The administrative system, with its high number of managers, may create stability, but its abundance surely does not create the added value companies are looking for. It is one of the reasons why administration has become a dirty word in the business community.

Every year, when – as a business school professor – I confront my (E) MBA students with the fact that they are basically administrators, responses are quite emotional. They range from "no way" to "how dare you say that ... we are leaders." It always takes a moment for them to realize that MBA stands for master of business administration.

After this realization has kicked in, I explain briefly why administration is being used in reference to their education and then quickly move on to make it clear that leadership is not simply a management position. It works every time to help set the stage and motivate aspiring businesspeople to explore their inner selves and explore ambitions beyond those that their formal (management) positions require of them. And, every time, my students realize that it is in that explorative journey where their leadership experience begins.

This anecdote reveals that too many people in business assume that a formal position with the title *manager* already implies leadership. We have become so accustomed to bureaucracy that many of us have convinced ourselves that administrative work as a manager already constitutes a form of leadership. Unfortunately, this is not the case.

Before diving deeper into why this is not the case, I do want to emphasize that management is not a bad thing. First of all, we cannot all be leaders, so being a manager is not something to be ashamed of. Management is needed to help provide an organization with a stable foundation. As a matter of fact, if an organization does not have this foundation to work with, we would not then see the emergence of those talented individuals that eventually take up leadership roles and promote innovation within the company. In other words, company goals can only be attained if we first lay a stable foundation.

Achieving more means less management

Once this foundation is in place, however, companies do need to create a culture in which employees feel inspired to elevate themselves beyond their formal job requirements and think outside of the box – this is the only way to bring the company closer to its future goals. And, it is in this latter part that the problems usually occur.

Indeed, a major problem today is that most people cannot move beyond the mindset of being a manager – they seem unable to elevate themselves. Rather, the administrative approach that most companies adopt seems to motivate employees simply to make management more perfect. As such, most of us are good at overmanaging. As managers we have become too accustomed to managing the work schedules of others full time, which means that, at the end of the day, everyone monitors others to stick to what we know and do.

If what I am saying here is the general attitude in today's business world, then we have a real problem. We have a problem because with an over-management mindset nothing will change and although change is not required all the time, when the time does arise we need to know that our company is ready to deliver. Such a reality also requires that we develop enough leaders to make such future decisions. Interestingly, the famous management scholar, Kotter, mentioned that managers are working in the here and now, whereas leaders are coping with the future and the possible changes they see that need to happen.[85]

Kotter's analysis is of great value to understanding why some companies are better prepared than others for the future. In fact, he is saying that when a company has only managers, a culture develops where pro-active thinking is not present because the focus remains on what needs to be achieved today (not tomorrow). Such an organizational culture breeds less creativity and innovation and is thus less likely to survive. As Kotterman noted, "when compared to a leader, the workplace manager is often generalized as an 'unimaginable clod.'"[86] I refer to companies with such a mindset as those where a management-only culture is at work. What are the consequences of such a work culture?

The danger of status-quo thinking

A management-only culture means that employees think and act in certain ways. They possess a very specific type of mindset that turns them into the perfect administrator.

What kind of mindset?

Because the narrowly defined purpose of management is to maintain order and stability, employees will primarily have an introspective attitude. They develop the habit of scrutinizing whether the administrative system works within the company and are therefore oversensitive to employees breaking rules. Maintaining the system is key! Such a mindset means that in their view the problems that need to be dealt with are urgent matters and, as a result, they invest all their energy in *fighting fires*. This ensures that nothing changes and thus prevents growth.

This is the problem with status-quo thinking. Is this such abnormal behavior? Not really. We know that people have a natural tendency to avoid uncertainty and stick to what is known. When we encounter a crisis, our first instinct is to try to return the situation to how it was before. We have a strong desire to believe in the saying that *we have always done it this way*.

Unfortunately, business today operates in a complex and volatile world, and we therefore need to adopt a more agile perspective to be able to deal with future changes. It is clear that a culture of status-quo thinking will fail in today's business context. Moreover, status-quo cultures are often overly complex and slow down decision procedures; they promote procrastination and poor communication across different levels within the company, which then become ambiguous and, hence, inefficient.

A status-quo focus also goes hand in hand with a *ticking the box* mentality. In order to maintain stability and prevent chaos, we implement procedures to achieve clearly-defined targets. The execution of those targets then become the primary focus. Put simply, the targets become the entire job description. If the targets are achieved, we pride ourselves on being an efficient organization. And, we are, from an inward point of view. Within the organization, people do what is being instructed and so everything is at peace. But, of course, does the outside word agree with this assessment? Indeed, the big question is, while a management-only culture increases internal efficiency, is it also successful in a volatile and complex business environment?

Targets make you blind to what really matters

If a company resorts to a technique where people simply have to comply with the wishes and demands of their manager, short-term thinking will prevail. Succeeding in the targets a manager sets out might then be executed without thinking too much about what these targets mean, how they can help the organization, or even whether the employee should try coming up with new ways of approaching the same task. What matters is simply achieving one's KPI, as soon as possible, without thinking on a long-term basis.

Can we expect other values, such as co-operation, building trust and sustainable ways of working, to be promoted if such a mindset is present? In my view, those values are less likely to surface and influence the behavior of employees. But, even if organizations decide that an emphasis is needed on those other values (beyond one's KPI), the pervasive presence of a management-only culture will quickly undermine any benefits that could come along with such an emphasis. Why?

What is typical in a management-only culture is the habit of transforming any new initiative into a new target. For example, I know of a company where the idea was fully embraced that storytelling promotes thinking and talking about the organization's values, and as such leads to greater commitment and engagement. However, what was initially meant as a tool to bring people together and make them think beyond their KPI became yet another assessment tool. How did this happen? Well, the manager demanded that each employee had to tell a story every month. If you did not prepare a story you were evaluated as disengaged. It only took a few months for this manager to transform the so-called *open work* environment into one that many felt was like working in a police state!

What is clear is that an excessive focus on management often reveals a culture in which change is experienced as a threat and therefore simply not rewarded. What is rewarded the most in these cultures is the achievements of targets that ironically contribute to the status quo. As I mentioned earlier, in such cultures one could even say that employees will be fearful of coming up with any new ways of working. Thoughts of changing anything are futile and if they turn out to be too disruptive, they may even be penalized. If such a philosophy becomes shared, thus creating a collective mindset, any employee – newcomer or old-timer – will quickly develop the habit of blindly following. This doesn't really sound like the perfect work climate to develop the leaders of the future, does it?

Any leaders out there?

Of course, we need employees to follow those in charge, because in an ideal situation, organizations undergo changes due to developments in the external world and, as such, actions have to be co-ordinated. But, if the culture does not promote creative thinking and co-ordination is mainly perceived as a way to keep things as they are, then followership will become mindless and enforced rather than empowered. People will follow, but simply because they have to (remember their focus on the targets) and they will not show any real engagement or creative thought that leaders need so dearly when engaging in any change project.

If you ask any manager whether they would like to lead teams of employees who think out of the box, bring creative ideas to the table, and pursue those ideas with a kind of entrepreneurial spirit that helps them achieve their goals, almost all of them will respond with a strong "yes". Sadly though, over-management in reality breeds a workforce with the opposite attitude. It breeds employees who do not think independently because the box is doing the thinking for them. The box says what is important and what they need to do. Management is only out there to follow up and reward the achievement of those given targets.

As a result, management-only cultures foster a climate where people have no judgments and because they have no judgments, they will not take responsibility for their actions. Even worse, they will not experience any ownership of their job. And, it is eventually this lack of ownership that creates employees who are not motivated to think pro-actively and avoid bringing new initiatives to the table, resulting in a complex organization where inertia is king.

Yes, management is needed, but more is required to ensure that the fostering of stability within an organization can be used as a strength, rather than a weakness. Building the foundation should be the first step and, as such, can be used as a strength that allows for room to be agile and creative with the ultimate ambition to grow as a company. As a second step, we would then need leadership to step in and help create long-term value. In fact, in an ever more rapidly changing world, we need more leadership and should not remain committed to over-management.

If we remain too committed to the management-only mindset, the imposed inertia among employees will lead to managers that increasingly fail to bring projects to a successful end. The reason for this is that, although we have created stable conditions to embark on a project, the reality is that throughout any project managers are confronted with disruptions and unanticipated changes and challenges. With a workforce that is not taught, even discouraged, to take the initiative and think differently, projects are likely to fail.

Leadership is not management

At this point, you must feel that the difference between leadership and management has become so clear that it is shouting in your face. Management fuels stability, whereas leaders take the company further and focus on delivering change. Leaders are the ones that communicate a vision. For many of you, vision is a buzz word that is used often, but which remains very ambiguous. How do you develop a vision? Well, a vision shows what can be achieved and what the desired end-state of the change process may look like.

Leadership starts with a vision!

So, leaders are therefore – by definition – not solely focused on the daily management of procedures, but more on enabling employees to do the future work. How do they achieve this? Leaders are expected to inspire others to join in with the change that is being proposed in the vision. Leaders need to empower their people and do so by providing a compelling message that points out the direction the company should take. A leader also explains why this vision, and the resulting direction taken, is the best one to take (given the circumstances being faced). In this sense, leaders add purpose to the vision they communicate. So, in a sense, leadership starts when management finishes the job of providing a stable work environment. Leaders inspire a ready-made workforce and institute a mindset of forward thinking.

Of course, for leadership to succeed, we must remove the mindset that management-only cultures install. Leaders can only motivate people to step forward and contribute to the purpose-driven journey when they are not fearful of thinking outside of the box. Leadership can only succeed if employees are not afraid to express their own judgment and ideas. It is only then that creativity blossoms and the future can become a point of attention.

When focused on a future vision, the purpose of the company will be much more on people's minds. To reveal this kind of thinking, it is important that, contrary to management, leadership is not a coercive process. It should not be bound to achieving immediate value through setting well-defined targets. Rather, leaders should portray change and disruption as catalysts for thinking outside of the box, as well as encourage transparency and install new ways of working.

If effective leadership is based on making followers think like this, what then can be regarded as the true essence of leadership? All of the creative and forward-looking attitudes are clearly meant to create a better future and thus serve the collective interest of the organization. Effective leadership emerges when leaders are able to influence others to embrace the purpose of the organization; to think and act along with the changes that are required to serve the interests of that same organization. So, leaders with no influence will not achieve change, and will not be able to promote either the short- or long-term collective interest.

Some leadership scholars made it their life's work to show that influence and persuasion are indeed key elements that make leadership work.[87] Put simply, leaders succeed in bringing change because they can influence people to work towards the change. Managers do not use influence in such a way. Rather, they have to resort to more coercive forms of influence. Managerial influence uses protocol to dictate what others need to do and assesses it accordingly. Of course, to be influential based on a vision and its associated values requires a leader that can achieve a sense of connection with others. Contrary to management, social skills are not a luxury but a necessity for leaders.

To establish this connection, leaders need to make sure that others think they can be trusted. Without trust, there is no leadership. When leaders have a clear vision and want others to engage with it, they need to be able to take the perspective of those they wish to persuade and use those insights to convince them that the vision represents their interests as well. If your employees perceive that you care about their interests and wish to align them with the interests of the organization, trust grows. So, trust facilitates influence and ensures that a vision is accepted. Once this happens, the leader can initiate the transformation needed to make change happen.

Of course, the collective goal goes beyond the individual interest of each employee. The trick is to make employees feel they are not only respected and included in the organization, but that their efforts are needed to achieve a goal that transcends the interests of all. That transcending goal is the purpose-driven direction the leader outlines in their vision. The leadership scholar, Bass, put it nicely when he argued that leaders "move followers to go beyond their own self-interests for the good of their group, organization or community, country or society as a whole."[88]

Not all hierarchy is algorithmic

Clearly, management and leadership differ in terms of their focus and way of working. In general terms, management requires a focus on the present, and works by evaluating targets and using a formal and rational approach to execution. It is conducted in a consistent way and is therefore easily replicable. Leadership, on the other hand, requires a more pro-active approach, as it focuses on future value to be created. As such, leadership builds connections with others that primarily rely on social connections, which implies a more emotion-based approach to execution, and because of this unique relationship with followers, is therefore less easy to replicate.

When looking at these differences, the attentive reader will probably start to see how and at what level algorithms may be applicable within the organizational hierarchical structure. In the following chapters, I will elaborate on this question by exploring more deeply how the algorithm fits within the management versus leadership framework.

CHAPTER 5
Bridging Management and Algorithms

COMPANIES TODAY HAVE become relentless data-processing machines. It is therefore no coincidence that the notion of big data has become such a buzzword in the business community. Companies have realized that they have so much in-house data available, which, if processed and analyzed properly, could drive revenue and make them more effective. Business strategies today then need to focus on data management in combination with evidence-based execution.

It is becoming clear that for contemporary organizations, data is a sacred component of performance management. In fact, data is increasingly being referred to as the *new oil*.[89,90] This increased focus on data is something that all of us are confronted with on a daily basis. Organizations require as many personal details as possible, communicate a wide range of targets to achieve and set out to assess those targets in a timely fashion. As a result, continuous evaluations and additional requests for supplemental data have become a routine process, revealing large data sets for each employee. The challenge for any *smart* company today then is to manage and connect all these data sets to optimize execution and enhance performance.

This reality has implications for our jobs today. First of all, due to an increased focus on acquiring data, most of us are becoming occupied with managing and updating our own data files (as often requested by the HR department) and documenting our activities. Second, all this data needs to be submitted on a regular basis to internal systems in the organization and will be used by our managers to evaluate our performance. This way of working obviously generates a lot of data, but most companies, eager to call themselves skilled in management of big data, consider this strategy essential to their reputation of being a smart company.

On the other hand, the entire process of managing and submitting data, which is then continuously evaluated and updated, also takes a lot of effort and time. This contributes significantly to additional layers of bureaucracy. Indeed, the fact that the focus on big data promotes bureaucracy in organizations, combined with the observation that companies are not necessarily good at using big data in effective ways, makes one wonder whether the whole obsession with data collection, evaluation and use is actually worth all the effort.

Presumably there must be an upside to this way of working. And there is, if we consider well-informed management as a key to an organization's health and prosperity. We all know that good performance is key for companies to compete and to survive in the long term. This managerial truth requires organizations to engage in performance management strategies rooted in updating, processing and evaluating the data of each employee. This way of working allows for managers to give feedback to employees in a data-driven way, which is believed to be more accurate and should therefore be more effective in making each employee perform better. Today's challenge for managers is thus to promote performance by making the best use of the data available. If management's aim is to promote stability, order and consistency in producing the best outcomes possible, then working with data is a key principle to optimize the management of any organization.

Do I need to become a coder?

When you read all of this, you may consider the thought that these data-driven processes, ultimately leading to more *optimized* performance management, run in very rational and consistent (even replicable) ways. If this is the case, a question that emerges rapidly is whether we really need humans to execute the data driven management aspects of an organization? In fact, if you are asking this question right now, you may have touched upon one of the most important questions in today's automation age: should management as we know it become a job performed by algorithms?

If the aim is to use data in more optimal ways to rationally and consistently empower better performance management, then humans may not be fit for purpose, especially not if the amount of data that needs to be dealt with is continuously increasing. To answer this question, it is useful to first look at the exact qualities attributed to algorithms and how they can help organizations run in more successful ways.

The one thing that makes algorithms uniquely fitted to any job related to data management is that they work so much faster than humans in collecting, evaluating and integrating data. Second, they work more systematically and are rational in arriving at conclusions (no sentiments or intentions are at play), making their predictions more impartial and accurate. And, finally, employing algorithms is way cheaper than hiring humans for the same job.

Putting all these qualities together, and assuming that any organization wants to drive down costs and raise up the effectiveness of execution, algorithms do appear to be a better substitute for human managers. Tasks will be done faster, at a lower cost and with a higher level of accuracy. It sounds like the ideal scenario for any business leader working hard to optimize the working of their company. In fact, in light of how management is defined in the literature (see the previous chapter) and the current trend to narrow down managerial work to mainly administration and performance management, we, as humans, seem to have put ourselves in a position where we can be easily replaced by algorithms. It should therefore be no surprise that voices exist saying that the end of human managers is in sight.

Algorithms clearly have the winning hand when it comes down to being the rational administrator for which we have long searched. In addition, because of their fast and consistent way of working, they are unbeatable in providing the most optimal use of any data available. It also excels in the practice of evaluating and even categorizing the performance of any employee. This reality has not escaped the attention of our managers today. In the last few years, I have noticed that in my (E)MBA classes, students almost immediately start sweating when they discuss the future of work and the roles of humans and algorithms. As I explained earlier, MBA stands for master of business administration. In theory, this categorizes any MBA student as an administrator trained to run companies in a systematic way, with the belief that management is based on rationality as a guideline. It is then no surprise that once these students realize that algorithms are designed to be much better in this kind of rational way of working, many of them worry about their future.

What is the value of being educated in rational business strategies by business schools if the underlying assumptions of those strategies can be better executed by an algorithm? Wouldn't it be a better investment for them to become a coder and leave the business wisdom to algorithms? After all, they could design an algorithm and be entirely in charge of it, rather than competing against the algorithm's rationality?

Does human intuition pay off?

Don't worry, as I explain later, there is no need to become a coder. There does, however, exist a need to train our business students in new ways, so that they are better informed on the application of algorithms and what it might mean for today's management. They also need to learn how to deal with this trend towards automated management by knowing which skills to focus on in the future. But, before I do that, let us be fair and see whether there are really no objections towards using algorithms as the perfect substitute for the human manager.

The initial response could be that as machine intelligence improves (and it is doing so almost on a daily basis), the more likely it is that humans will lose this debate. So, rather than focusing on whether humans can withstand the rise of algorithms in management positions, wouldn't it be better to shift our focus on the unique human abilities that algorithms do not possess. This revised focus may help us to get a better picture of how management will change by means of automation as well as what role humans will play.

So, what traits can be considered uniquely human? Interviewing managers who have worked in recruitment for several decades, many point out to me the importance of human intuition. Some of them have developed a kind of sixth sense that when looking at a CV they immediately *feel* whether this person is suitable or not. For those who have been in the recruitment industry a long time, their predictions are usually pretty accurate! Since it is essential for a manager to ensure good performance, they need to be able to bring in the right kind of people. Indeed, recruiting and finding the right fit between the new hire and the organization is an important management responsibility. And, if human intuition seems to be important in this, could it then be that the human side of management still has a shot at surviving? But, before we answer that question, let us first try to understand exactly what human intuition is.

Is human intuition really such a mysterious feeling? Unfortunately, to those who like to believe so, behavioral science has made clear that intuitive decision-making appears to be the result of training, although a kind of training of which one is often not aware. How? Well, there is a reason why I emphasized that the intuition of long-term recruiters is often accurate in predicting positive hiring decisions. Day in, day out, for a very long time, they have been doing the same task. As a result, they have so much experience with all kinds of situations that their brain is trained to know immediately what to do and what to expect. Over the years, a recruiter will build up, both consciously and unconsciously, a multitude of relevant information. And so, many years down the line, a recruiter's intuition will have become like a fine-tuned instrument – an almost perfect recruiting tool.

However, recruiters who have been in the job for only a short time may know the requirements of the job and what information to look at, but their intuition is unlikely to make them successful. This is because they did not have time yet to train their brain in unconscious ways to make the best decisions possible. Furthermore, even for those very experienced recruiters, the positive influence of their intuition is still limited. Indeed, simply ask these very experienced recruiters to make a quick decision in an area different from their own expertise and their intuition will not be that effective.

The human sense of intuition as a powerful tool to optimize predictions is thus very much expertise related and takes a long time to perfect. Importantly, for those non-recruiters reading this book, looking at intuition as a subconscious process works in similar ways across any job in business.

My favorite example to demonstrate this assumption is to refer to the workings of company boards. I always ask my students which team in their company is the one that makes decisions almost always in intuitive ways. Usually, I get responses like the sales team, R&D, customer management and so forth. When I mention the board of directors, some look up in surprise while others cannot suppress their laughter, as if they are immediately recalling board decisions that were flawed by what we call human intuition. Is this such a surprise?

If we look closer at how boards usually make decisions, it is interesting to observe that in the decision-making process many board members overly rely on their sense of intuition. Many of them even explicitly say that their *gut* feeling is the advisor they trust the most to make important decisions. The reasoning behind this is always that they have the idea that their intuition helped them to get to the position they are in now, so, it is the best predictor for making good decisions. As a result, if something does not feel good, they vote against it, but if it feels good, they vote in favor. The reason for them to rely so much on their intuition is simple. Across the many management positions they have held over the years, they have acquired experience in all kind of business decisions. They have experienced and seen the outcomes of those many business decisions and have internally built an image and feeling that they have seen it all.

The brain plays an important role here. In a way, their brain has – on a subconscious level – stored all this experience, all the data, acquired during the course of their career. So when, after many years as board members, they are asked to make the ultimate decision, the stored information in their brain speaks to them via the magical process of intuition. This is the reason why their gut so often talks to them. And, because they literally feel it (or, at least, in an imagined way), they also trust it and consider it to be true.

The human brain shines, the algorithm gets things done

So, the process of intuition teaches us that humans can actually become pretty reliable and accurate data-processing machines. And they can use their acquired knowledge as input for the decision-making process. If this is the case, then why bother to automate management? Isn't it the case that what algorithms do today is essentially the same process?

Algorithms quickly assess, analyze and connect the different pieces of data and start self-learning (just like humans subconsciously process experiences and learn from them). The way algorithms work ultimately enables them to identify trends that help bring transparency to complexity and increase the accuracy of predictions. The rapid advancement of AI is based on our increased insight into how the human brain works. As such, it is clear that algorithms are modelled on how we think the human brain approaches and analyzes information. The only big difference seems to be that algorithms work so much faster – humans clearly need many years for their intuitive sense of accuracy to kick in. Given the fact that algorithms are modelled after the human brain, it should also not be a surprise that we are thinking of applying algorithms to the work performed by humans. In organizations, this will first and foremost include administration and performance management.

Before we move on to see how grandiose and beautiful the algorithmic side of management may turn out to be, I would quickly like to note that by drawing a parallel between the human brain and algorithms, I am not claiming that the human brain is something that is not advanced. In fact, as we strive to replicate the human brain, people may even get the impression that the organ is not such a *big thing* after all. Well, let me make this clear to you: the human brain is a big thing!

If you talk to any neuroscientist, psychologist, or brain scientist, they will all tell you in the most beautiful way just how magical and complex the workings of the human brain are. And the reality is that today, in this respect, our technological advancements are just not that advanced. This is especially apparent when it comes to the potential for technology to truly understand how human intelligence operates.[91] To expand further, the human brain is so complex that we actually still know very little about it. For example, we still do not fully understand how the electrical signals of neurons influence the brain's functioning, something which is key to the learning and associative-thinking process. Besides this, our methods to examine all of these internal brain functions are far from perfect.[92]

Although we know far less of the human brain than we would like, technology develops quickly and the benefits of applying it are growing every day. As such, these advances force us to be serious in thinking about automating management. Even though we are not yet able to develop algorithms that capture the complexity of the human brain, many managerial tasks can actually be done by algorithms in much faster and more accurate ways. Many companies work in volatile and fast moving environments. Under such circumstances, most companies do not have the luxury to train humans to become the perfect manager. They do not have the resources or the time to employ managers for so many years, just hoping that at the end of the day they will deliver the perfect result.

And why should they? Just think about it. If you have algorithms ready to jump in to perform the basic management functions in more optimal ways, why hesitate? Take, for example, the management of recruiting. In this field, evidence is mounting that algorithms are already producing better results – despite not having the sophisticated intuition of experienced human managers available. The paper from the National Bureau of

Economic Research that I referred to earlier corroborates this idea. This paper examined the employment record of 300,000 low-skill, service sector workers across 15 companies. In this sector, workers usually leave their job quickly (they stay for an average of 99 days). Interestingly, however, when an algorithm was involved in hiring these workers, they stayed in the job 15% longer.[93] Findings like this clearly indicate that algorithms can bring immediate added value to job performance.

Obviously, the enormous cost benefits and immediate value created has not escaped the attention of the business world either. It is therefore no surprise that today we see strong signs that the traditional management job is under threat from algorithms and there is a global trend towards automating management functions. This is especially true for managerial functions that include a focus on data input and maintenance. Processing is also expected to be automated in the near future.

Data management is needed to facilitate the use of the correct type of data to co-ordinate projects effectively. Performance should then increase accordingly. Interestingly, surveys reveal that on average, managers spend 54% of their time on exactly those kind of administrative tasks.[94] As algorithms are the real experts when it comes down to working with data, automation of these functions is taken for granted. In fact, most business leaders believe that it is a given that administrative jobs will face massive replacement by algorithms. This is not simply a prediction for the future, it is something that is already happening today. Examples abound: IBM, for example, applies the algorithm Watson Talent to its own HR teams to promote speed, efficiency and the optimal use of their operations.[95]

Another example of such automation is the use of Robotic Process Automation (RPA). RPA uses software algorithms to closely replicate repetitive tasks like moving data between two spreadsheets. And, finally, especially within the context of HR management, the employment of algorithms to conduct repetitive administrative tasks has already been proven to be effective. For example, every time a company hires a new employee, algorithms can automatically update data files, including vacancies; create accounts for the new employee within the employee system; and integrate the software systems so the data of the new recruit can be accessed by different departments across the company. All of these examples show that today the automation of administrative tasks is mainly focused on the facilitation of repetitive and routine operational decision processes.[96,97,98,99,100,101]

Bring out the blockchain

OK, algorithms are executing managerial responsibilities, but that does not make them managers. Does it? Maybe algorithms are not real managers yet, but what all these examples demonstrate is that companies are not just thinking about building a work culture of automated management, they are already doing it.

Increasing amounts of evidence suggests that the practice of automation will not only be limited to simple administrative tasks that can be executed in efficient and fast ways. In fact, the trend to automate management roles will gradually involve more complex jobs, such as evaluating human employees to facilitate more effective collaborations and exchanges at work. Algorithms will not only be used to document and analyze personal data, but also to monitor employees by collecting new data that could complement the data collected when those employees were recruited. For example, algorithms are already monitoring the time you spend on the internet, your whereabouts within the company and even your health data.[102]

Yes, algorithms seem to be assuming the role of *big brother* and, as such, seem to become the manager that we know today. The contemporary manager evaluates and monitors your progress and performance. In light of this movement of algorithms into a role of managing (some may say monitoring) others, an interesting application in this area concerns the potential employment of blockchain technology to manage work relations in organizations.

Blockchain is mostly known as the underlying technology of applications, such as Bitcoin. At the same time, the technology is also increasingly being seen as a way of changing how our companies work. One specific application that was pointed out in a recent Deloitte survey is to use this technology to perform the basic functions of management as well as motivating employees more specifically.[103] This survey revealed that among 1,386 senior executives in 12 nations, 83% saw compelling ways for blockchain to be used by their organizations. Of specific interest to our discussion here is the finding that 86% of these executives believe that blockchain technology can be applied to the aspects of management that involve leading an organization. How could blockchain technology be used to achieve this goal?

Let us first consider, what is blockchain? Blockchain is a distributed database composed of a chain of blocks in chronological sequence. Each block is a collection of data. Blockchain records data about past behaviors of individuals who are all participating within the same interconnected network. The technology behind blockchain thus builds a platform that holds a transparent and immutable record of past events relevant to all individuals within a shared network. This network could be a team, department or even the organization in its entirety. Transparency is created based on the history of interactions taking place within the network, which means that a blockchain should have the ability to make individual parties trust each other. Indeed, in 2015, *The Economist* put blockchain on its cover and called it "the trust machine". Because of its supposed ability to create trust, it should be possible for blockchain to manage behavior within companies.

The key element in blockchain's supposed role as the trust builder is that it creates a *risk-free* environment. The past of every individual involved in the network is controlled and the risk of exploitation is therefore virtually zero. When it then comes down to managing an organization, blockchain technology is regarded as suitable for delivering assurances (a stamp of verification that interactions are safe) that can increase co-operation, while protecting individual employees' interests from exploitation. With this set-up, many believe that the ability of blockchain to provide total control will help increase feelings of safety, and, hence, trust.

Isn't that what managers should be doing in the first place? If so, technology like blockchain will indeed become part of our management systems very soon.

Management by algorithm

But, to answer the question of whether the algorithmic manager will wake up soon, let us return again to how we defined management. As I explained earlier, the purpose of management is to ensure that order and stability is maintained. According to our initial analysis, algorithms seem perfectly equipped to achieve this purpose. Indeed, as all the examples illustrate, algorithms penetrate managerial jobs by providing more specific and consistent ways of assessing, monitoring and evaluating employees.

Today, algorithms are able to learn about employees in fast and accurate ways, and can make valuable and reliable predictions regarding the future behaviors of those employees. As such, algorithms do possess the necessary skills to execute many – if not most – managerial tasks. It is at this stage that we can say that management by algorithm has become a reality and will only grow further in importance in managing our future workforce. Management by algorithm is not a fantasy anymore, it has arrived and is likely to stay.

The next steps in allowing algorithms to penetrate management functions are already being prepared. At first, we saw algorithms capable of executing monitoring functions at large, but today, we are already moving into a more complex reality where algorithms can take over actual managerial decision-making roles. Along with an increasing technological sophistication, which allows algorithms to learn on their own (without human involvement and supervision), algorithms are gradually replacing human resources to increase efficiency of execution and productivity. One example is that algorithms are moving more gradually into advisor roles. In this role they provide feedback on how human employees have to interpret data analytics and what those interpretations mean in light of the decisions that have to be taken. Take for example, the situation where algorithms are being prepared to analyze the skill sets employees need to perform in the organization of tomorrow, but at the same time also make suggestions on the appropriate pay levels for the employees that they evaluate.

At this point, you may say: hold on, the influence of algorithms may technically be possible, but will we simply accept their advice? As I mentioned earlier, people can be OK with algorithms making decisions. In some cases, they may even prefer it, because algorithms are not seen to have their own intentions and therefore their decisions are considered unbiased.

So, overall, the involvement of algorithms in managerial decision-making clearly brings benefits to the table and, interestingly, we may well be ready to accept this. At the same time, however, we have to remain aware of where the limits lie in accepting algorithms as a decision-making tool. But, why should we be aware of those limits? Isn't it a good thing that algorithms bring more objectivity into our decision-making and, as such, relieve humans from making tricky decisions where the risk of damaging the interests of others is high?

True, increasing the objectivity of any decision is a gain. But, by placing algorithms in a role where they are the ones deciding on the interpretation of the data, the risk exists that once we do not understand anymore how the advice comes about, we are not simply guided by algorithms, but led by them. Indeed, if we reach a point where algorithms are self-learning, to the extent that we do not understand any more why certain decisions have to be made, we will have given the responsibility of decision-making to machines.

Being responsible for a decision also means that we need to make sure that the interests of all stakeholders are served. In other words, the responsibility of decision making lies in being able to make the right judgment calls to ensure any value created contributes to the welfare of others. If algorithms can grow into this role, we need to be sure that they will make human-centered choices which respect the welfare and protect the interest of humans. After all, if algorithms reach the point of self-learning and decision making, we have little or even no latitude to correct.

The limits of management by algorithm

Because of these reasons, I feel that we need to think not only about the unlimited potential for algorithms to make decisions, but also about where we set the limits of an algorithm's decision-making authority.

As I will discuss later, algorithms are limited in taking the perspective of a human and understanding the deeper emotions that underlie the human ability to make judgment calls. But, aside from the fact that algorithms do not have a real understanding of what the human condition entails, they are also vulnerable to certain errors and biases that could violate respect for the human identity. As a result, algorithms may possess the ability to optimize decision making, but a lack of empathy and understanding of what it means to be human will increase the risk of omission errors, in which alternatives that are more human-centered may be discarded.

For these reasons, we need to decide on how best to regulate self-learning technology, which implies deciding on where the limits of management by algorithm lie. Although humans also display biases, we are usually aware of them and have the ability to empathize with those being treated unfairly. Hence, a human would likely try to correct the situation. As algorithms do not experience such compassion, their more accurate, even superior, decision-making abilities will not allow them to identify biased implications towards human actors.

Indeed, growing evidence suggests that algorithm-based decisions amplify human biases in the data they analyze. The problem is that while humans recognize a bias, algorithms do not, because they learn from observation and observable trends. The meaning and emotional connotation behind such trends will not be recognized by an algorithm and thus, decisions will not be assessed and revoked when necessary. For example, in 2018, Amazon applied algorithms in their hiring decisions and discovered that the algorithm gave higher scores to white males.

So, the algorithm was making decisions in favour of white humans who were male. How is this possible? Well, the algorithm learned from historical job-performance data and recognized the trend that in the past white men had been the best performers. Humans obviously know that in the past the majority of those employed were white men, but that norms regarding diversity in society has now changed. It is humans who have that emotional awareness, but algorithms do not. Hence, it does not make them able to make judgment calls. Of course, as I mentioned earlier, humans are also capable of making biased decision, but because of the human ability to create meaning from different perspectives, remedies and solutions can be identified. It is therefore no real surprise that as soon as Amazon identified this problem, the company stopped using the system since there was no simple way to fix it.

So, where do the limits lie of management by algorithm? The first conclusion is that many, if not most, managerial tasks that fit our definition of management will become automated. Management represents a way of providing a stable work environment and algorithms can execute most of these tasks. Does this mean that we can then simply delegate the responsibility of managerial tasks and decisions fully to algorithms? No, it does not. What we can learn from Amazon's failure is that execution of management can be done by algorithms, but not without human involvement and oversight.

Increased speed, heightened accuracy and replicability of decision outcomes is a very valuable addition to the management process, and algorithms are the ideal candidates to perform such tasks. But, when it comes down to making decisions where different human-stakeholders are involved, companies need to realize that the interpretability of the decision-making process is more important than the skills algorithms bring with them. Indeed, decisions need to be put in context and interpreted in light of different perspectives. As a result, algorithms cannot move into autonomous management roles where they assume full responsibility for decisions made.

Co-operation is the key word

Management by algorithm is a reality, but it is constrained to the automation of managerial execution efforts. In addition, managerial tasks and decision making that does not impact the value of the company may, over time, also be delegated to algorithms. All of this also makes sense in light of how companies want to position themselves in the market.

Think about it. If we see automation of management becoming possible, and in this process we decide to delegate increasingly more responsibility and authority to algorithms, then all of us will eventually adopt similar approaches to the data out there. As a result, we will increasingly make similar decisions, which will lead to the reality that companies become almost replications of themselves. Running companies in unlimited automated ways will therefore increase the likelihood that all those companies will become interchangeable! However, is business not about being able to create value based on unique priorities and strategies that distinguish you from the competition? Yes, it is.

If we are afraid that automation of our management will make us dependent on what the algorithm delivers, then we put ourselves in a position where we look at companies as passive recipients of automated authorities, spitting out data-driven advice. Unfortunately, no passive company can be creative, forward looking, and create value for society and the stakeholders it serves. The reality is, if our organizations were to be run in this way, then it is likely that we may destroy many beautiful assets and resources (e.g. a collaborative, trusting and empowering work context), compared to organizations led by leaders with clear values on how to deal with different stakeholders.

Some of my own recent research points out this possible failure.[104] In a series of experiments, we placed human participants in a work context where their task performance was assessed and evaluated by an autonomous algorithm. The evaluation of the algorithm was used directly by the top of the company to reward the participant. No intervention of a human supervisor was possible. No possibility was given to participants to express one's view or feelings towards human supervisors. We also created another condition where an autonomous algorithm performed the same assessment, but this time our participants could talk to a human supervisor and share their experiences. What we found was that in such an automated performance context, human participants considered the work context to be more trustworthy and fair when human supervisors were involved. This was particularly the case when those supervisors were also perceived as being humble (and thus value-driven).

What these results indicate is that, in a context where algorithms engage in the managerial task of conducting performance evaluations, employees feel that human leadership with strong values is needed to create a sense of fairness and trust in how the organization as a whole operates.

Although the reality of management by algorithm makes it clear that management functions are likely to be replicated by algorithms, it also makes clear where the future of human management lies. That future is in the domain of leadership. It appears that when automation goes up, so do a number of other factors: our need to have leadership in place that knows what it wants to achieve; leadership that offers judgment when decisions have to be taken; and leadership that can reflect effectively on the goals to be pursued.

Data is all well and good, and can point out several directions to take, but the final, strategic decision lies with human leadership. Because of the unique human capabilities, the direction a company takes ultimately always needs to be based on what is valuable to the business, their customers and society. The reality of running an organization in the future will be that the more algorithms take over management, the more we will need leadership to bring in human judgment to help set priorities. If this is the case, then we see a similar story emerge, as we did in the past, where we emphasized that the running of an organization requires managers and leaders to work together to create both innovative and sustainable ways of doing business.

In today's business climate, we again see this pattern emerge through algorithms taking care of management and humans accounting for the leadership responsibilities. This idea indicates that the way to run organizations in the future will be to follow a collaboration model, where algorithms and humans jointly create value. As Kevin Kelly in his book, *The Inevitable*, notes: "This is not a race against the machines ... This is a race with the machines."[105]

CHAPTER 6
Algorithms and Leadership

ORGANIZATIONS CONSIST OF data. Business executives use that data to come up with the right strategies to best serve the company's interests. As we said before, and I will repeat again: data is king!

But, what does data say? Can data speak?

Yes, on some level we could say that data speaks because, if algorithms can create transparency, then data provides useful information about what is going on. Hence, I have argued that algorithms will move into management as they will manage the data available. But, what about the other question: can the management of data to create transparency also be seen as leadership? Can data management by algorithms also lead? If this is the case, then algorithms will not only provide advice (based on the data analyzed), but also move into the role of leader, where they will make strategic decisions.

In my view, this is not very likely to happen. Why? Well, data carries information with it and, if analyzed well, we can see trends emerge. For this reason, algorithms can easily take the position of an advisor, but it becomes a different story if the information provided needs to be interpreted in line with values and priorities set by humans (and that underlie the strategy the company should take). As you all know, in our daily lives, we are raised and encouraged to have a set of values that can help us to make (difficult) decisions. In a similar vein, in organizational life, values also matter, as they help to set priorities in the projects the company engages in. It is the pursuit of those values that makes the execution of a project meaningful.

Having the feeling that what you do is meaningful is important to *who* we are. Meaningful experiences make our lives worthwhile and are therefore greatly valued and pursued. So, if in all areas of our life we strive to do things that make sense and can be considered meaningful, then benefits must exist which arise from those actions. One such benefit is that it makes us feels authentic. We feel close to ourselves when we see our values being represented in our actions, and therefore we truly feel like the person we would like to be. In other words, we need our decisions to be motivated by authentic goals and values, because it is those projects that we consider as important to what we do. It is those projects that feel like the real deal.

The need for this specific authentic sentiment has important implications for the question of who can and should lead in an era where algorithms are increasingly taking over the management of organizations. Indeed, at the end of the day, any decision taken by organizations where human employees are involved, should ensure that it is motivated and inspired by what feels real (from a human point of view) and not by an artificially created and directed reality. In light of this requirement, it is clear why it may not be a coincidence that when we talk about automated processing and decision making, we refer to *artificial* intelligence, and when we talk about human-driven processing and decision making, it may be more appropriate to refer to *authentic* intelligence.[106]

Both types of intelligence can be captured by the same abbreviation, AI, but they are *not* the same. Yes, both artificial and authentic intelligence can be considered to have influence within groups and organizations. However, it must be at different levels, because they clearly cannot be interpreted as having the same level of authority. In other words, artificial intelligence will be driving management, whereas leadership will need to be driven by a sense of authentic intelligence.

Why leadership needs to be the real deal

Authenticity of thought, being able to think and act in line with our values, has been considered by scholars as a key aspect of effective leadership. How so? Well, it all starts with our expectation that leaders be the agents of change.

We expect our leaders to inspire and motivate people, so that they can create value in their actions for the collective. This collective value is created if a leader can point out the direction a company must take (what to do) and explain why this is the case (introduce a compelling vision). If a leader with those abilities is in charge, he/she will be more effective in motivating and inspiring others to move in a new direction to create more and better value in the future. It is for this reason that scholars have argued that leaders need to possess transformational qualities, allowing others to be willing to collaborate to make change happen. So, the ability to transform a given situation into a new one, by means of inspiring others to follow your vision, is key to effective leadership.

Now, is the algorithm or the human best equipped to achieve such a process-based form of leadership? Academic research on transformational leadership – regarded as the prototype of effective leadership – may provide the most direct answer to this question. In fact, the initial writings on the idea of transformational leadership emphasized the importance of authenticity, if a leader wanted to be successful in motivating their followers to create value and perform better.[107]

Indeed, an abundance of studies have shown that leaders who act in an authentic human way, through being genuine, purpose-driven and able to connect with others, are truly transformational in their efforts. Thus, effective leadership clearly requires an authentic sense of intelligence to facilitate understanding of what really matters to people and their interests. This knowledge can, in turn, be used to motivate them to deliver value-driven change. From this point of view, the human, rather than the algorithm, seems to fit the bill. In fact, by being more specific about the process that makes leaders effective in their job, we are able to identify the limitations that are likely to prevent algorithms from assuming an effective leadership role.

Leaders influence people in value-driven ways, so the collective can benefit and long-term value can be created for all. Such kinds of influence are not achieved if leaders only present facts. Influential leaders motivate people to act and people are most likely to act if what the leader says and asks makes sense to them. They will act if what is being presented to them (the facts, a vision) is meaningful to them.

To achieve such types of influence, leaders need to be able to truly touch people's hearts and make a *human* connection. Leaders thus need to know, first of all, what is happening and what changes are required to be successful. But, to make such changes happen, they need to be able to connect with their followers. Such a connection requires leaders who can communicate what is being asked by using the perspective and values that the others will recognize and endorse. In other words, leaders may know what their organization needs to do to survive or remain competitive, but the action will only be delivered if they have the skills to make it meaningful and appealing to others.

Looking ahead with a sense of purpose

Algorithms may provide information and advice on what the present business situation looks like, allowing us to infer which actions are needed, but algorithms do not possess the skills to, first, recognise what that information means to a company populated by human employees and, second, communicate in authentic ways, so that others are inspired by the message that change needs to happen. These *human* requirements can be easily identified when we look at the circumstances under which leaders nowadays have to perform.

What is typical of today's business environment is its complexity, which is shaped by high levels of ambiguity and volatility. These characteristics require leaders to be agile in how they run their organization. Leaders are expected, on the one hand, to know about and adjust to the rapid changes happening and, on the other hand, be able to keep a focus on the company's priorities. In other words, leaders need to be able to understand and use the purpose of the company to make the right strategic decisions to create long-term value.[108,109]

If leaders only make decisions that solely respond to updated information about changes in the market (possibly provided by algorithms), then we cannot say that the company is being led, but rather managed. A company is only being led if updated information is made sense of and responded to in terms of the purpose of the company. This means that even though an analysis may indicate that a company should make a change, a leader may reject the advised option because it does not align with company values and stakeholder interest. It is this kind of reasoning that is needed to allow leaders to connect with their employees.

Indeed, to make the required action meaningful, a leader must have the ability to understand the short-term challenges and put them into a broader perspective where the purpose of the company and the interests of all stakeholders, including employees, are accounted for. It is this ability to focus on facts and emotions, almost simultaneously, that makes a leader truly inspirational.

Can algorithms bring this *human* ability to the table?

Algorithms can help with the first step, which is to provide accurate updates on what the facts say and even what this means in terms of the available options. But, making the actual choice by accounting for *why* it is the case that the company and its employees hold certain values dear, to ensure that employees follow the direction of the leader, is a somewhat different task.

True, algorithms can make very good predictions based on the data available, but if these predictions are the only basis for the decision being made, then the decision itself is only responsive and based on short-term concerns. Effective leaders, who are able to bring the change needed to create real long-term value, are not only responsive but primarily act in pro-active ways.[110] Pro-active thinking is exactly the skill that combines the power of analytics (knowing and understanding the facts) with the ability to think in the long term and in this process, to imagine the value that could be created.

Qualities such as imagination, value-based thinking and strategic vision (short term versus long term, the concerns of different stakeholders) help leaders to connect to others in ways that help them to embrace the change requested. Indeed, deciding to follow a leader in often uncertain circumstances takes people out of their comfort zone and brings emotions, such as fear and anxiety, into the picture.

Leaders need to have the skill to show empathy and recognize the fact that followers will experience those emotions. Therefore, leaders need to be able to nurture their followers into staying motivated and engaged. For this to be successful, leaders are required to be intuitively attuned to these emotion-based dynamics.[111,112]

Our own research shows that we do not believe that algorithms can possess these abilities.[113] In one study, we asked participants to evaluate the qualities of a human versus an algorithm, to understand the meaning of relationships between humans. Not surprisingly, our results revealed that humans were judged to be more intuitive, as well as better able to understand the perspective of another person and act upon it accordingly. Algorithms, on the other hand, were judged to be less qualified when it came down to these skills, mainly because they are seen as rational decision-makers with no sense of intuition.

It's all about connecting with others, stupid!

These findings support the message that algorithms cannot connect with humans in the way another human can. Connecting with humans requires the ability to install a somewhat authentic feeling that emotions are understood and values shared. Algorithms lack these social skills and, as such, emphasize the reality that they are non-human and thus cannot act in authentic ways. Though this conclusion is a simple one, it carries important implications for the ability of algorithms to ever take up a leadership position.

Effective leadership materializes only if the kind of influence achieved allows others to follow. True leadership, in its essence, requires the ability to connect with those who are expected to follow. The fact that algorithms do not possess such abilities, nor are perceived to have those abilities, makes them incapable of leadership. Even more so, it makes thinking about leadership by algorithm, leadership that would be responsible for the interests of its human followers, a scary idea to many.

Being responsible for others indicates that one is judged as morally capable to evaluate and understand the interests of those you are leading. You need to have a sense of intuition that is morally-laden, if you want to lead. Academic research shows that we do not attribute these qualities to machines in leadership roles because we do not regard them as having a *complete mind*.[114] You may wonder now, what makes for a *complete* mind?

To understand this, let's take a look at how research defines the human mind when it comes down to morality. As I mentioned briefly earlier, a range of studies has revealed evidence that in our perception, a human mind entails the two dimensions of agency and experience.[115,116,117,118,119,120] Agency is the capacity to do, to plan and exert self-control; whereas experience is the capacity to feel and make sense of things.

Algorithms may be attributed some agency, although this is still an issue where no consensus has been reached. For example, the EU recently published ethical guidelines for a trustworthy AI which was criticized because people believed that AI cannot be trustworthy. The reason for this claim was that AI is considered not to have agency. My own research on trust would suggest that this is not entirely true because we do seem to be comfortable with trusting algorithms to do what they can do best, that is, to be rational and deliver fast accurate analysis.[121] In this sense, algorithms can be seen as reliable, but this is not the same as being trustworthy. Being trustworthy also involves acting with integrity and being aware of the interests of others. (For more insights on what building a trustworthy image entails, see chapter nine.)

One thing that is, however, clear for the algorithms that we have developed today is that they do not possess the benefit of experience. And because algorithms are not attributed with both dimensions, humans feel uncomfortable letting algorithms make decisions that have consequences for the interests of different stakeholders. Only a leader who possesses authentic, human, mental capacities is expected to be able to do this.

Failure happens; what matters is, can we correct it?

Does all of this mean that humans, relative to algorithm, are flawless when it comes to taking care of the interests of others? Of course not! We know all too well that humans make moral mis-judgements and show unethical behaviors. But, contrary to algorithms, we perceive and accept that humans do possess both agency and experience. And because we perceive humans to have these abilities, we also trust them more than algorithms to correct misbehavior. Algorithms do not have the ability to authentically feel and experience what others go through when being treated badly, or when their interests are violated and forgotten about. Even more so, their inability to take the perspective of others makes them unable to make decisions on behalf of others and, as such, are perceived as incapable of leadership.

Let us consider again Amazon's experiment to use an algorithm to automate their recruitment process. This case taught us that the employed algorithm duplicated the human bias to favor men over women for the specific software development jobs they were advertising. As I just mentioned, it is not just algorithms, but humans too, that make such biased judgments. The difference is that humans are aware of the social consequences that emerge from the employment of this biased practice. The important question here would therefore be whether algorithms could sense the dangers associated with these consequences. Clearly, they did not. The algorithm did not say, 'wait a minute, is the outcome of my decision what we would like to see in the company and hence society?' Not at all. It took human intervention to change the selection process.

This example makes it clear that if we decide to make ourselves dependent on automated technology to lead our organizations, we would almost certainly face consequences that would be difficult for humans to accept. Algorithms can make data transparent and even provide advice, but it cannot be allowed to take charge of the decision-making process.

All of this signals that algorithms can be used to manage the execution of our (value-driven) directives, but not create such directives. If we employ algorithms in this way, it will mean that humans are better able to direct their attention towards more complex, higher-level responsibilities. Workplace culture, as a result, will be better able to foster moral awareness, creativity and innovation. And at the end of the day, isn't this what leadership should really be about?

Does it make any sense?

The verdict seems ready: leadership in today's world, and especially so in the future, needs to be driven by an authentic human sense of intelligence to be effective. If we want to follow up on that advice, we also need to know what dimensions this kind of intelligence includes. In other words, which unique skills do humans bring to the table to make them the undisputed business leader of tomorrow?

If there is one aspect that addresses the core functions that business leaders will need to fulfil in the future, then it involves *sense-making*. Organizations today and in the future will face very complex situations, combined with a volatile market that requires leaders to make decisions quickly and accurately. To do this, it is necessary that sense can be made of the organization's goals, as well as why (its purpose) and how they can be achieved within a business environment characterized by these unique features.

Leaders help define the organizations they lead. Therefore, those same leaders need to make sense of what they are doing and more importantly, why they are doing it. This helps employees to make sense of very complex situations for which no formal rules (yet) exist. We all know that once things become complicated and more difficult to cope with, we look in the direction of the authority to guide us. We did so when we were children, and we do the same at work. Humans have the innate need to look for help from their leaders when things get tough. This reality clearly emphasizes that leadership is more about responsibility than many assume, hence, making moral awareness an imperative. Unfortunately, too many times we hear about leaders thinking about their job more in terms of what they are entitled to, rather than recognising the responsibilities that come along with their leadership position.[122]

Leaders can and should provide guidance to others, but it very much requires them to have the ability to create meaning for those who they lead. For this reason, the ability of sense-making has to be recognized as an important quality for the leader of tomorrow. The ability to make sense corresponds to the specific intrinsic desires that make us human and, in this way, sense-making adds value to our lives. What unique human skills make up for this general ability to make sense of things? What skills can be located within the human brain with its 200bn neurons, connected by 10,000 synapses, which is impossible to replicate even with today's technology?[123]

Unravelling complex situations so that they make sense to others implies an equally complex working of our brain. It implies that leaders need to be able to bring different perspectives to the table, understand the meaning of those perspectives to the stakeholders involved, and are both creative and integrative in producing a solution that creates most value (not only in financial terms but also in terms of purpose fulfilment).

This complex interplay of abilities represents an image of the human skill-set that aligns well with the skills that the World Economic Forum (2016) identified as being needed to deal with the technological revolution that we witness today. Specifically, their *Future of Jobs Report* emphasized that humans in the near future need to be able to solve complex problems, engage in critical thinking, act creatively and be equipped to manage people.

On the fabric of sense-making

It is the interplay between abilities that creates sense-making value, which only humans can deliver in a leadership role. Put together, these abilities form the skill set required for future leadership to succeed. But why are these abilities so important?

To understand their unique value to the leadership of tomorrow, we need to understand the psychological fabric that makes up for the sense-making ability of a leader. This fabric consists of a number of well-defined abilities. How does each ability work in making a leader more effective? Understanding the specific abilities that are seen as important to the overall skill of creating meaning are obviously important in order to develop more effective training and coaching of our future leaders. So, where do we start? What is important to realize first is that these abilities are not all operating at the same psychological dimension. Specifically, each ability is a combination of a desire to create meaning (*motivation*), to be able to think about it (*cognition*) and to realize how it makes people feel (*emotion*).

The existence of these psychological dimensions already distinguishes humans from algorithms in terms of the complexity of their behaviors. Indeed, as I discussed earlier (see chapter one, the Turing test), algorithms arrive at their decisions (and hence behavioral displays) in a less complex way. They only reason in one specific manner, which is learning based on what they observe. In other words, algorithms learn and subsequently model the behavioral trends that they identify in the data they analyze.

For example, the chip-maker Nvidia recently introduced an experimental vehicle based on an algorithm that had taught itself to drive by observing how humans drive. Thus, the algorithm learned through behavioral observation and subsequently modelled the most consistent behaviors. Yet the algorithm did not engage in any reflective, motivational or emotional analysis of what driving means for the drivers.

As the Nvidia example demonstrates, algorithms are not able to think at a deeper level, where motivations and emotions are integrated with a cognitive analysis to make sense of things. An algorithm's way of learning is thus less complex when compared to the complex interplay between neurons and synapses in the human brain. Therefore, their resulting actions and decisions can be considered straightforward and rational, as it is based on principles of consistency and replicability.

If there is one thing that effective leaders know, it is that every individual is unique yet desires to be affiliated with and treated in the same way as others. This complexity requires leaders to integrate emotions, motivations and cognitions into their judgments and act accordingly. It is exactly this kind of thinking that we need to see present in leaders in the 21st century. Such a conclusion implies that leaders of the future require the human touch that can bring to the table the abilities of critical thinking, curiosity, agility, imagination, creativity, ethical judgments, emotional intelligence and empathy.

Figure 1 illustrates how a leader's crucial skill of sense-making is derived from a diverse set of abilities that operate on multiple psychological levels (motivation, cognition and emotion). Below, I discuss each ability in greater detail.

Figure 1: Abilities driving the skill of sense-making as required for leaders of the future

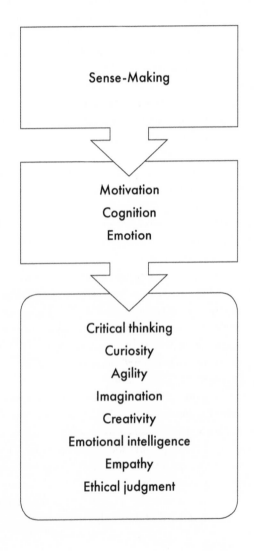

Critical thinking

When confronted with complex situations, it is necessary to identify where the opportunities for your company lie. Where does your focus need to be in this complexity? What kind of information do we want to use and which can we ignore?

Obviously, algorithms can help here as they gather and analyze data faster than any human. They are the masters of managing complex information! So, it is only justified that we use them in this way. However, there is so much more about data that needs to be considered. What purpose are we striving for and what kind of data is needed to inform us about the opportunities we can create to achieve that goal?

Algorithms run on calculative principles, so humans need to assign weight to what matters more, versus less, to help categorize and bring structure to the data. It is the ultimate goal that gives meaning to the data search and subsequent analytical process as conducted by the algorithm. We therefore need leadership to be able to reflect and consider this critical issue. But this is not where critical thinking ends.

Once the relevant data is identified, we also need to analyze it in terms of the strategy that we need to develop, based on the demands imposed by the business environment. So, we may have our purpose and our own view of reality, but there is also a reality out there with its own specific demands. You need to take the latter reality into account too if your company is to survive in the long term.

All of this requires leaders to be able to think outside of the scope of the provided data and make connections others (i.e. competitors) may not see. It also requires the ability to think logically to evaluate how the results (as achieved in a competitive and demanding market) relate to what you want to achieve and why. This logical component of thinking is essential, because not every successful business scenario is necessarily the right one. The ultimate business scenario at the end of the day is the one that optimizes the achievement of your purpose. Not every company is in business for the same reason, so they are not necessarily focused on creating the same kind of value. Algorithms lacking the emotional connection with what brings value to people's lives do not engage in this kind of analysis.

Finally, critical thinking skills are not only necessary for leaders to use, but also to install in the company's work culture. Leaders build work cultures by setting examples and instilling values for which the company wants to be recognised. In this sense, a leader who practices critical thinking will also equip their followers with the same skill. After all, as we will see later, employees will work with algorithms to optimize efficiency in the operations and execution of tasks, so they need to be able to manage these processes in the same way that the leader manages the direction and purpose of the company.

Curiosity

Your ability to think critically is linked to another human (cognitive) drive, which is called curiosity. Curiosity is one of the new buzz words in management today. In fact, curiosity is a leadership skill that many business leaders are starting to consider a key quality in today's volatile business environment. Why would that be the case?

Dan Shapero, vice president of Global Solutions and head of sales for LinkedIn, put it succinctly in an interview when he said, "Leaders need to understand and interpret the massive amounts of data that are coming at them every minute of every day and be able to cut through the noise ... We have to be able to ask questions that focus on what this all means for our business, our customers, and our teams. This puts a premium on having people who are driven by a sense of curiosity."[124]

And, indeed, organizations driven by a curious attitude perform better. Curiosity is a strong predictor of employee performance and, in combination with the skill of critical thinking, becomes a powerful (human) weapon in producing valuable outcomes for the company. What is important to note is that research shows that it is curiosity in *general* that makes people successful and not simply a sense of curiosity in a *specific* task.

In his book *Originals*, Adam Grant, professor at the Wharton School of the University of Pennsylvania, elaborates on this general/specific issue by pointing out that Nobel prize winners have a greater sense of curiosity beyond their own field of expertise than scientists who are less accomplished. The study he refers to looked at every Nobel prize-winning scientist from 1901 to 2005 and examined their hobbies and ways of expressing themselves creatively. The surprising result was that scientists who showed great engagement in hobbies like art, music and so forth, had 22 times more chance of winning a Nobel prize.

What do these results really suggest? Well, these findings underscore the observation that it is really a general level of curiosity that determines the success of a person, rather than curiosity in a specific area of expertise. This general sense of curiosity brings a more critical and refined way of looking at what happens around you to the table. It is especially this kind of attitude that allows curious people to think beyond what they see and come up with more creative solutions.

Without curiosity, leaders are less likely to get better at what they do and will be deprived of useful information that can help them grow and improve the effectiveness of their organization. According to the Cambridge dictionary, curiosity is defined as an eagerness to learn about something. Being curious promotes learning and motivates people to improve themselves in many dimensions of life (both professional and personal).

Why does it improve learning? Curiosity pushes people to think outside of the box. It makes them attentive to the fact that there is more than one solution for a problem. A wider range of solutions exists! This awareness motivates people to look for new possibilities, to explore different ways of approaching decisions and to challenge beliefs that they have held for a long time. Curiosity is the primary challenge to status-quo thinking. It is not expected to be part of the manager's job (see chapter four), but should definitely be considered a part of a leader's job!

The judgment of the jury in this is clear: curiosity helps people grow, encourages them to learn new things and enables them to develop into more creative decision makers. Curiosity is a motivational driver that comes from within the individual. This implies that to develop this ability, you have to make it happen yourself. No one else can really do this for you. We all know that dealing with complex and uncertain situations creates a tension within people that makes them feel uncomfortable. Depending on the way we regulate this tension, we may either grow and perform better, or become paralyzed and stick to the status quo. The one feature that decides whether you end up in the former situation and not the latter is curiosity.

Why? Being curious implies that you realize you do not know everything. Fortunately, though, you also realize that there are plenty of opportunities around to learn; it depends on you whether you take those opportunities or not. It is in this explorative process that you are likely to find a solution that fits with who you are, what you feel comfortable with, and which will allow you to grow. Having an open mindset and being curious about how things can be done differently brings with it the power of imagination, which fuels new and creative ways of dealing with business challenges. Being both curious and critical in your thinking creates leadership that acts in agile ways.

Agility

It is no surprise that a famous business rule is that the only thing unchanged is change itself. Indeed, in today's business environment, situations can change quickly. And with this change comes different expectations and demands. Organizations need to adapt quickly, but without losing sight of the goals and purpose they wish to achieve. No organization is helping themselves if they only follow what others do and in essence become a purposeless company. To avoid this fate, agile leadership is needed. Leaders are required to improvise and find new ways of acting quickly. This, in turn, requires strategic thinking, which allows an organization to remain on course to achieve its goals while at the same time being attentive to the new business requirements.

Agility is typically a human quality that algorithms do not possess. Great examples of the limited ability of algorithms to be agile can be found in the gaming industry. We can make algorithms learn the ability to play a video game like StarCraft II up to the level that they beat the best human professional players. But, if we change just one parameter in the game, the algorithm has difficulties adapting immediately and will lose again. Algorithms cannot step out of one situation and into another unfamiliar one. Because of the fluid business environment, organizations face these types of changes frequently and so would not be able to survive without agile leadership.

Agility requires (like curiosity) an open-minded approach which quickly recognizes that the old ways will not work anymore, so new solutions need to be found. To find those solutions, agility is required. Agile leaders are able to take different perspectives towards the changes they are facing and, combined with a sense of curiosity, are energized to find an alternative approach that will resolve the challenge faced.

Taking different perspectives implies that leaders have a sense of imagination and can see new ways of working that do not yet exist. Leaders therefore need to be curious and adopt different perspectives simultaneously, which is encouraged by having a strong sense of imagination. To make things even more complicated, all of this has to operate in a quick and seamless way. To achieve such a state of mind, leaders are required to train themselves in taking different perspectives and adopt a reflective (where multiple options are considered) and integrative style (where the different perspectives are integrated to reveal one solution that is considered optimal given the situation).

Imagination

Fluctuating business conditions induces the need to work in new and different ways. At the same time, you cannot change the values that underlie your drive for performance, so you adapt but without compromising your values. What makes this process so complex and difficult to attain is that it requires decision making and action that basically does not exist yet. It requires the ability to mentally simulate the probable success of adopting new business models and strategies. This distinctive ability concerns the power of imagination and is an ability most required when something you are looking for is invisible or does not yet exist.

To engage in mental simulations, you need to have the right set of abilities. Indeed, you need to understand how the game has changed (critical thinking); stimulate yourself to look for new solutions (curiosity and agility); and combine the information you already have with the additional information you need to successfully deal with the new challenge. This latter aspect of combining what you know with the things you do not yet know is the ability to imagine different realities.

In its essence, imagination is the dynamic process of filling up the gaps, i.e. the gaps that exist in-between the pieces of information you have at your disposal need to be filled up by other new data to construct a more comprehensive and different way of working.[125] What is important to understand is that this imagination process implies that in order to find the new information, you will have to look outside the framework that you have always been using. When both types of information (the known and the unknown) are put together, it needs to be done in such a way that it is not a simple extension of your old ways of working! Instead, it needs to reveal a new and different way of operating that fits the changed reality that now confronts you. In this sense, 1 + 1 = 3. The process of imagination and how to stimulate it is receiving increasingly more attention because, for obvious reasons, it is one of the primary determinants of creativity.[126] As the American Heritage Dictionary mentions: imagination can improve the ability to "deal with reality by using the creative power of the mind".

Creativity

Can you be creative without imagination? Not really. For most of us, imagining different realities is a fun activity. When we experience stress, we often retreat to our own imaginary worlds and think about alternate realities that make us happy. Humans have this unique ability to entertain themselves in the world we call imagination. This ability, which distinguishes us from algorithms, is very important when it comes to creativity. As Einstein once said, "creativity is intelligence having fun", and all of us understand immediately what he meant by this quote. Algorithms cannot be creative because they work with pattern recognition and curve fitting, which does not allow for the exploration of a reality that does not exist. It thus seems unlikely that algorithms have the same ability as humans to solve creative problems.

Creativity is a process that requires imagination. As creativity involves coming up with new ideas and solutions, imagination is required to, first of all, develop different ways of looking at reality. In those different perspectives, we try to identify opportunities that can generate novel solutions to problems. Creativity is therefore regarded as a key enabler of tremendous advances in organizational productivity and economic growth.[127] However, creativity does not only produce novel solutions, but also ones that are useful, which is vital for organizations in the context of a fast-paced business environment.[128] The fact that creative solutions also need to be useful is important to stress in light of the human ability to make sense of things.

Creative solutions are meant to solve problems that hinder the pursuit of our goals and achieve results that we consider appropriate in light of our purpose. Because creative solutions are so closely aligned with the value that we want to create as humans, the *aha* moment that precedes the creative idea is felt physically, emotionally, and mentally. Creativity in itself is such a deep and authentic experience that the process does not function within a controlled and structured operational mode. Algorithms – in their effort to model the human brain – function on a set of well-defined calculative principles. Their way of working is modelled after insights from the field of computationalism, which simplifies the workings of the human brain and associated thinking process to some arbitrary act.[129] This kind of algorithmic formalism does not leave room for chaos and, as such, does not allow for any expression of the human experience of creativity.

Does this mean that algorithms cannot provide any input to the process of creativity? Not at all. If we look at scientific literature, we see that creativity can be reached via two paths: flexibility and persistence.[130] Flexibility is associated with an open mindset that helps people to adopt different perspectives; avoid being pinned down in looking at reality in a fixed stereotypical way; and connect unrelated concepts and ideas. Persistence is more structured and includes diligent work, systematic thinking and exploration, and knowledge-building in an incremental linear manner.

Looking at these processes shows some parallels between what humans and algorithms can do. Algorithms are rational data processors that systematically work through massive amounts of data, as well as generate transparent and consistent pieces of information – a way of working that fits well with the notion of persistence. Algorithms are persistent (and fast!) in processing data. Humans, on the other hand, possess the ability to be more chaotic, blend in emotions with their thinking and deviate from a systematic and consistent way of working. These are all abilities that make thinking less fixed and more flexible.

What do these scientific insights teach us? First, the definition of creativity makes clear that a creative outcome ultimately depends on the notion of flexibility, because a creative solution needs to be something new. As such, truly creative solutions will always require human input. It also means that algorithms, because of their persistence, can assist the creativity process by helping to gather and make data more transparent. This, in turn, will provide humans with the necessary input to unleash their chaotic and unpredictable processing mode.[131]

Emotional intelligence

Anyone who has been in a leadership role knows that your decisions impact others, as well as yourself, on many levels. In the last decade or so, calls have become very loud for organizations and their leaders to become better at nurturing employees and showing some empathy. For leaders, this includes taking care of both their own emotions as well as those of others. This implies that leaders should be able to recognize emotional disturbances. This ability to recognize emotions (both in themselves and others) and manage them to reveal a positive impact is called Emotional Intelligence (EI).[132]

In line with this call towards nurturing emotions within the organizational setting, it has been estimated that demand for EI skills will increase by a factor of six in the next few years.[133] The world has clearly woken up to the fact that our business environment creates stressful lives. Although the awareness seems to be there, organizations have not always been responsive enough in terms of fostering the ability to develop and use EI. This may be considered surprising, because EI has many positive influences in the workplace.

Research reveals that employees with high EI are consistently rated as more dedicated to their job, better performers and easier to deal with.[134] These findings underscore the idea that EI is a valued social skill because it facilitates how you interact with others in the most optimal and beneficial ways. Indeed, EI can help you to understand others, take different perspectives and regulate your social interactions with others. Those who have a high level of EI have a high sense of self-awareness (they know their strengths and weaknesses). They are also able to recognize their emotions and manage them (e.g. use fear in a motivating, rather than a destructive, way). Individuals with a high EI can thus put their emotions into perspective and use this ability as a strength to help them be more effective and perform better.

If algorithms will be the new co-workers, then we need to be able to collaborate with them. EI is an ability that many technology companies hope to integrate within AI. Indeed, new technologies will gradually automate more routine tasks and eventually make the leap to decision making within the context of managerial responsibilities.

If an emotional AI can be achieved, leadership may become automated after all. In light of these predicted developments, having algorithms equipped with some kind of EI ability will likely transform the future work setting, making it even more effective. In addition, because many jobs will increasingly become automated, employees will, in a way, be forced to re-discover their ability to connect with other people.

Indeed, as algorithms take over the more analytical jobs, humans will be more in demand for jobs that deal with other humans. For example, in the financial sector, banks are gradually replacing human employees, particularly those with jobs that are largely mechanical and calculative, with algorithms. This is an obvious trend, because now AI is rapidly advancing, thinking tasks that require analyzing and processing data can be easily automated. It makes sense then, that some bankers today will proudly state that they are not banks anymore, but rather technology companies with a banking license. This development creates a reality where human employees have to start focusing on the tasks that algorithms are not able to do, those jobs where social and emotional skills are a priority: the *feeling* tasks.[135]

This shift in focus for humans is seen more and more in job advertisements, where banks will emphasize the need for employees to have strongly developed social skills. In fact, some of our own research suggests that wealthy clients in particular seem to demand more face-to-face interaction the more automation kicks in. As such, relationship management will become a crucial job within the financial industry. In a similar vein, management of the work force will require *people managers*. This is not such a surprise, because within such a tech-driven environment, it is actually quite a normal *human* response for both employees and customers to need more social contact.

So, both algorithms and humans will engage in their fair share of jobs, but, at the end of the day, they will have to collaborate to create value. From this perspective, developing algorithms able to deal with the emotions of customers and employees would be highly beneficial to organizations. However, if we look at the current state of affairs, then it is fair to say that machines cannot recognize human emotions beyond the surface level. They may recognize an emotion, but they do not have the qualities to understand what the person expressing this emotion is really feeling and what this means. At the same time, research has revealed that algorithms cannot feel authentic emotions, limiting them to make sense of those of others in a way that signifies real understanding.[136] Put differently, at this moment in time, developing algorithms equipped with EI is not possible. Hence, algorithms and machines cannot be attributed human qualities, especially not those needed to lead people in appropriate, respectful and empathizing ways.

Empathy

EI implies the skill of emotional recognition. But why would you need to be able to recognize emotional states? Well, to connect with others and develop relationships with them. So, is EI sufficient for the relationship to happen? Not entirely. We need something more. Specifically, we also need the deeper-level ability of being empathetic. Empathy is the capacity to understand the implications of the emotions people experience. What is it that people are feeling behind their emotional expressions? Why does someone experience these emotions? Showing empathy helps to develop a better understanding of *who* the other person is, and the kind of joy and pain they may experience.

Empathy is believed to be uniquely human, as it helps us to accept another person with the emotional weaknesses and strengths that they display. Algorithms, on the other hand, run on well-defined calculative principles aimed to optimize outcomes, which means that their functioning does not need the ability to dig deeper than the surface of the data that is available. As such, algorithms do not have the ability to engage in the process of obtaining a deeper understanding of the external environment, let alone accept that environment.

This limitation is nicely reflected in comments by Bill Mark, president of information and computing services at SRI International, whose AI team invented Siri: "We don't understand all that much about emotions to begin with, and we're very far from having computers that really understand that. I think we're even farther away from achieving artificial empathy." Of course, if empathy cannot exist between human and algorithm, then it is difficult to talk about the possibility of developing trusting partnerships. After all, empathy would involve mutual recognition of one's feelings, which would lead to the existence of mutual trust where both parties can genuinely take care of each other.

Ethical judgment

The use of algorithms has clear financial benefits, as they cut costs dramatically. Of course, this will only be the case if algorithms are used in ways that suit their abilities. Replicating routine tasks, being consistent and predictable, and interpreting data, for example, are all fine. But, organizations have to make many decisions that are more complex and involve the ability to be sensitive to the interests and values of other stakeholders.

In this sense, many business decisions need to be evaluated in light of upholding important ethical values. Indeed, business leaders need to be aware of possible ethical dilemmas inherent in business decisions and possess the ability to judge how to deal with it. Specifically, to make the morally *right* decision requires the leader to make an ethical judgment. This is where algorithms fail, and humans bring their unique abilities to the table. Because algorithms lack empathy, humans consider them to not possess the full range of human qualities and are thus limited in their ability to make moral choices.[137]

Consider the following thought. In theory, it is the case that any machine can be fed a set of ethical principles outlining a clearly defined set of values and operate on those values. But, what does this set of values really mean to an algorithm? Can algorithms understand the meaning of a value to people, to organizations or to society at large? It is not always easy for humans to grasp the real meaning of values and incorporate them into their behavioral repertoire. So, how easy would it be for algorithms that lack empathy to understand the meaning behind those values? How can an algorithm decide what a universal right is to humans if it cannot imagine and feel what such a reality actually means?

Algorithms can learn and scrape the internet to see how people look at ethics and apply it in their lives. However, these efforts remain abstract and do not allow for an algorithm to grasp the meaning of why people value ethics. So, they can scrape ethical values, but not grasp ethical meaning! What can we learn from this thought exercise? Well, no matter how powerful an algorithm is in dealing with all the data available, it doesn't change the fact that all technology is neutral. It does not feel, shows no empathy and cannot understand the meaning of a moral decision to the different stakeholders involved in business decisions.

So, algorithms lack the ability to arrive at ethical judgments and are therefore considered unfit to make leadership decisions. Furthermore, because morality is an authentic feeling unique to humans and our society, people only consider human ethical judgments to be legitimate. In fact, recent research shows that people consider algorithms (as compared to humans) to exhibit less moral authenticity.[138]

What makes humans then so much more suitable to make these moral decisions? Compared to algorithms, humans are equipped with a sense of moral awareness. Moral awareness can be considered the innate level of sensitivity and responsiveness that humans possess to recognize that a given situation has a moral component.[139] To have this kind of awareness, one needs to be aware of the needs and goals of all the stakeholders involved to delineate whether a conflict of interest exists.

For obvious reasons, such a sense of awareness requires complex and integrated reasoning that algorithms are not able to achieve. Having a sense of moral awareness is critical for engaging in ethical analysis, judgments and finally conduct.[140] Indeed, we know from research that ethical judgments guide ethical intentions and behaviors.[141] And, it is this link between the ability to engage in ethical thinking, and to act in line with the corresponding ethical judgments, that makes it so unique and separates what we can find in a human from what we do not find in an algorithmic leader.

Leaders with the ability to think through the ethics of a situation are better equipped to make sense of a situation. By being able to recognize the ethical requirements of a situation, the meaning of that situation becomes clear and the appropriate response becomes apparent. Leaders with this ability do so by explaining the ethics of the situation, what the expectations are and how one should behave.[142] By conveying ethical expectations, leaders do what they are supposed to do: they guide their followers and encourage them to pursue the company values.

All of this makes clear that the moral complexity that comes along with doing business does not translate easily into the workings of an algorithm. To put it briefly, based on what we have seen so far, two important problems arise. The first problem is that multiple philosophical perspectives of ethics (e.g. justice, relativism, egoism, utilitarianism, and deontology) exist, which influence an individual's ethical judgments. This reality indicates that humans themselves differ among each other in terms of how they define ethics. This also means that some people will, for example, consider lying as something that should never be allowed, whereas, for others, lying is acceptable if it helps to avoid harm to others. Why is this a problem for the possible ethical development of algorithms?

Well, let's assume that we want to develop an automated work place where algorithms act in consistent ways across locations; such a set up requires that algorithms define ethics in similar ways. So, ultimately, for algorithms to achieve this developmental stage, humans would need to reach a consensus on how to define ethics first. To complicate things even more, the second problem is that, because algorithms cannot feel empathy, they fail to be morally aware. Thus, algorithms lack the ability to arrive at ethical judgments and make decisions in situations where multiple stakeholders are involved.

Given all these constraints that prevent algorithms from making ethical judgments, we are confronted with a new problem. Now that organizations are showing a commitment to creating strong, automated work environments, how can we be assured of the presence of an ethical compass guiding this automation trend? It is clear that the most adequate response will be to have human leadership in place to assess the ethical standards of any automation effort from a human-centric perspective.

Are companies aware of this need? They are. This awareness is obviously being helped by the fact that when it comes down to the development of algorithms to make decisions, the law is lagging behind and regulations cannot keep up. As such, it is hard to avoid the idea that one should not simply focus on compliance, but more so on having leadership in place that builds a culture of *doing the right thing*. Why wait for regulators to catch up with technology development, if leadership can also model the right kind of behavior?

Because of this awareness, it is no surprise to learn that in a Deloitte survey of 1,500 US executives, it was found that 32% of organizations considered ethics a top priority. But, although some awareness seems to exist, few companies have developed procedures to bring ethics training to life in the management of AI. So, more work is needed there.

The companies that do act on this challenge, however, approach it in a specific way. For example, companies like Microsoft, KPMG and Google, create internal positions that guide the use of algorithms within the company context. The senior leaders placed in these positions work with ethics frameworks to supervise how the technology is used in both efficient and ethical ways. These positions are now being called AI ethicists.[143] The company KPMG identified this position as one of the top five positions needed to succeed in 2019.[144,145] They stated: "As ethical and social implications of AI continue to unfold, companies may need to create new jobs tasked with the critical responsibility of establishing AI frameworks that uphold company standards and codes of ethics. Initially, these roles could be fulfilled by existing leaders in an organization, but as the effects of AI fully take shape, it may need to be the responsibility of one person to ensure these guidelines are upheld."

Conclusion

With all these unique human abilities present and ready to be developed further, it is safe to say that the art of leadership will not change that much. It will remain human. Yet, it must also be stressed that the automation trend is not to be reversed. So, the question of how to use technology and for what purpose will only become more important. When this happens, leaders will need to be able to make decisions based on the data delivered by automated management, but with a clear sense of consciousness, responsibility and sense-making.

CHAPTER 7
The Day that Empowerment Changed

I<small>T HAS BEEN</small> said that no two humans are alike. When it comes to leadership, we do not expect the next leader to be a replica of the previous one. However, when we talk about the trend to automate our organizations, the idea of replication is often raised. Indeed, algorithms learn and observe what the most consistent trends are and act accordingly. Algorithms therefore aim to replicate the best procedures available. This means that they can be more accurate (due to a reduced error rate) and faster to reach a conclusion than any human. But is the running of organizations really just about promoting replicability and consistency in operations and performance management?

To some extent, we do like replicability and consistency in our actions. Most humans are averse to uncertainty and feel more comfortable when things are predictable. In a world driven by financial incentives, humans also like to cut costs and the employment of consistent procedures helps to achieve that goal. Humans also do not like to waste time. Time is money and this is especially true when it comes down to leading people. Many leaders are put under pressure to avoid spending too much of their time on developing their own people to the sacrifice of financial gains. When reading all of this, we may conclude that algorithms could well be the answer to these three issues.

However, as we have seen so far, the most effective leaders do work differently. They appeal to a completely different set of human needs and values to transform companies into organizations that act wisely, responsibly and in line with their purpose, while creating value for all their stakeholders. Wise leaders critically evaluate the decisions that need to be made in light of different perspectives. They are driven by curiosity and are able to imagine how to deal in creative ways with problems. It means that wise leaders are aware of their responsibilities and as such try to treat all stakeholders fairly and respectfully.

This kind of leadership requires a range of abilities that we consider to be uniquely human. These are skills that algorithms cannot deliver, making them less suitable to replace humans in their leadership roles. Parry and colleagues (2016), for example, noted that "while automation of organizational leadership decision making might improve the optimality and transparency of decisions by organizational methods, important moral and ethical conundrums remain unaddressed" (p. 573).[146] And, von Krogh (2018), emphasized the important value of our unique human qualities by stating that, "In the long run, outsourcing 'intelligence' to machines will neither be useful nor morally right. Although such technologies have many attractive features, they merely emulate cognitive processes and cannot substitute the great flexibility, adaptability, and generativity we associate with human intelligence" (p. 408).[147]

Empowerment makes the world go round

We expect our human leaders to make meaningful decisions for the future in light of any given situation. The best way to assure that others perceive your decisions as legitimate is to connect people's personal experiences with the reasons why you have decided to act in a specific way. When people can connect to what you have decided, they will internalize the direction taken and support it. To achieve such an emotional connection, leaders need the abilities identified in chapter six. When leaders use those unique human abilities in effective ways, they are said to be able to empower others. Interestingly, decades of research shows that leaders can facilitate how meaningful people perceive their job and are motivated to do well, by empowering others. Empowering leadership provides others with a sense of autonomy by including them in the process of decision making.

Empowerment also enhances people's self-esteem, confidence and sense of control over the execution of their job. These are all outcomes at the level of the individual employee that need to be nurtured by our leaders. These days, we work in volatile and complex business ecosystems, and the increase of automation further adds to this complexity. As a result, people today, perhaps more than ever, experience uncertainties, loss of control and anxiety. Leadership, therefore, has never had a greater responsibility to empower and ensure that their teams are motivated to deliver high-quality, innovative solutions.

Interestingly, with the introduction of algorithms, teams will be composed of humans and algorithms working together. A consequence of this new work reality will be that leaders need to be better equipped to empower both humans and algorithms. What might such empowerment look like?

Leadership empowers humans

Empowering human employees so that they can manage their work environment better and improve their performance is a crucial leadership requirement. This need for empowerment will become even more important in an age where employees interact with autonomously-working algorithms. With the introduction of algorithms as a new co-worker, the psychological experience of human employees will become more complex. Leaders of tomorrow need to account for this and should be informed on how to empower human employees in this new age (see Table 1).

Table 1: The empowering abilities for humans by the leaders of tomorrow

Empowering ability	Actions taken
Managing aversive emotions	Reduce emotions of fear and anxiety Eliminate feelings of uncertainty Avoid feelings of loss of control
Managing distrust	Avoid power struggles Increase transparency
Managing technology education	Make leaders tech savvy Promote continuous education
Managing employee's expectations	Promote contact opportunities Create feelings of familiarity
Learning to explain the how and why	Be sincere Provide legitimate reasons Provide adequate reasons

1. **Managing aversive emotions**

One consistent finding that academic literature reveals is that humans are not very eager to prefer algorithms' forecasts over those made by humans.[148] Generally speaking, humans assign more weight and importance to human input than to algorithmic input.[149] As we saw earlier, this tendency for people to prefer human input over algorithmic input – even if the latter input proves to be more accurate – is called "algorithm aversion."[150] This aversion for relying on algorithms is somewhat irrational because, in specific tasks, algorithms actually perform faster and more accurately than humans.

A smart human should then surely be motivated to use the information generated by an algorithm to its own best interests, right? Well, we *do not*! In fact, people act quite irrationally – especially when situations are experienced as new, uncertain and complex.[151] Within the automation age, leaders therefore see a new empowerment challenge emerge, which is to manage the irrational judgments of employees towards the operation of algorithms in their work setting.

Why aversive?

First of all, we need to realize that algorithm aversion is real and motivated by irrational behavior. For example, if algorithms perform equally well, or even better than humans, then the range of solutions they identify can be considered useful. However, people will discount these ideas more easily when they find out they were offered by an algorithm. As a result, none of these solutions will be used. This example teaches us that our biased attitude towards algorithms carries the significant risk of making us less informed, and hence, less smart.

We lack open-mindedness in those cases. But, unfortunately, it is open-mindedness that drives creativity. And, this is not where it stops. Imagine what will happen to those employees who do comply with the advice offered by algorithms? Well, research shows that if the bias of algorithm aversion is a shared mindset within the company, then these employees may risk becoming stigmatized and even excluded from the team.[152] These findings clearly underscore the need for leaders to guide human employees more effectively (and less irrationally) in their interactions with algorithms.

But how do they do that?

Leaders will have to devote time and energy towards carefully assessing whether this aversion exists within their team, and, if so, where it originates from. Understanding this root cause will be helpful, since leaders will then be able to present a counter-argument through which employees can see the benefits of using algorithms. This will challenge the team perspective and hopefully ensure that team members become more effective and make a more significant contribution to the organization as a whole.

Tackle the fear

What are the reasons for algorithm aversion to exist? One reason is that most people are basically afraid of algorithms making autonomous decisions. An algorithm is a different kind of animal and, as such, is a relative unknown. Not being familiar with algorithms makes people feel uncomfortable. It leads to their being fearful about this new work situation. And with fear, comes uncertainty; whenever people feel uncertain, they distance themselves from the source of their fear. It is this kind of psychology that makes humans avoid or even discount the input of algorithms in the decision-making process.

The uncertainty experienced with respect to algorithms is particularly related to feeling uncomfortable with a new colleague who is not human. Just think about it! As humans, we have a strong drive for our society to adhere to human values, and, therefore, for decision makers to bring human qualities to the table. This is obviously not the case when we talk about algorithms. This technology does not have feelings and, in our view, is unable to address and deal with human experiences.[153] Hence, we would rather avoid this new co-worker.

Leaders therefore should be trained to minimize the fears that impact their employees' work experience. One way to do so is by making algorithms more human. Ensure that digital transformations are not simply executed because *everyone else is doing it*. Companies being motivated in such a way have usually not done their homework and are unable to assess the true value that algorithms can bring to the achievements of the company. It is therefore no surprise that many digital transformation processes fail.

In fact, digital transformations are more likely to succeed if organizations can help their employees to have a clear understanding of *how* and *why* algorithms should be used. Leaders thus need to better explain the use of technology to their employees. Creating a well-informed workplace allows a company to make better use of the best technology to fulfil their own unique purpose. Because, really, if the technology used is not up to the task, then there is no point in automating the workplace, since it will not bring any advantage. In fact, it may result in disadvantages, as employees will not engage out of fear of the new technology.

Tackle loss of control

A second reason underlying algorithm aversion is the fact that by allowing algorithms to be involved in the decision-making process, humans experience a loss of control in their job. The need to control one's environment is considered to be one of the most basic concerns known to humans.[154] People value control in almost all aspects of their life – especially so when decision making is involved. The concern to feel in control is so strong that people are even willing to make financial sacrifices, up to the level that it hurts their own financial wellbeing.[155]

In fact, my own research reveals that employees are willing to sacrifice a large part of their work budget to keep algorithms out of the decision-making loop, so that they can stay in control.[156] Obviously, such behavior is detrimental to the functioning of any organization.

We do not want our employees to use their work budgets to avoid using digital improvements. When this happens, employees devote less time to their job and underperform because they lack resources. What we can learn from all of this is that leaders in the 21st century need to become better at managing the emotions of employees when algorithms become their new co-workers. In this process, the unique human abilities of empathy and emotional intelligence will play a very important role and therefore need to be inculcated.

2. **Manage distrust**

One problem raised by using algorithms as advisors is that we will not always know why advice is offered or how a conclusion has been reached. People shy away from using algorithms because they think of them as a black box. No matter how optimally designed the advice may be, if we do not know how the advice came about, humans quickly withdraw and have doubts about it. We do not consider advice to be legitimate if the procedure behind it is unclear.[157] It is only when a source is considered legitimate, that results are easily accepted and used.

With respect to the use of machines in our work setting, the issue of distrust is a major one. Companies may be equipped to explain what kind of data is used and what kind of calculative principle the algorithm runs on. But, this is where, at best, it stops. What exactly happens *inside* the machine is unknown to most of us, and if it is known, it is often very difficult to explain. It is therefore no surprise that one of the major difficulties that companies experience is communicating the use of data.[158]

So, if we do not know the internal workings of the algorithm, how can we be sure that the advice is right? Even if the machine seems to be very accurate in making predictions, the lack of transparency turns it into a black box that humans have difficulty trusting.[159] At the heart of the problem lies the fact that humans find it difficult to trust algorithms as advisors. Relying on the wisdom that with knowledge comes power, algorithms being perceived as a black box will create work situations in which people will attribute power to the algorithm because only the machine knows (not the human!). Under those circumstances, people will feel they are losing ground to the algorithm.

It's all about power

With such a power struggle lined up, humans are likely to stand firm and discount the advice offered by an algorithm. The well-known example of IBM trying to use its supercomputer program, Watson, to help doctors diagnose and treat cancer (called Watson for Oncology) is a good example of this phenomenon. Watson was also seen as a black box, which led doctors to arrive at some peculiar conclusions. When Watson arrived at the same diagnosis as the doctors, they judged the program to be useless (it was not adding anything to what we already knew). When the computer program, however, arrived at a different conclusion, then doctors reasoned that the program was wrong.

You may ask yourself now, why did the doctors not think that *they* were wrong?

We know from research that humans have the tendency to evaluate themselves in more positive ways than others. Such a self-serving tendency is definitely more likely to occur when a human is compared to an inhuman entity. So, it happened that the doctors clearly considered their professional experience to be more reliable than the advice provided by Watson. And, of course, this helped them to be confident and trust themselves above the machine, whose internal workings were not even transparent.

Create transparency

So, what to do? Leaders need to create a feeling among employees that they do not have to be engaged in a power struggle with the algorithm. This can be achieved by opening the black box. By making the internal workings of the machine more transparent and easier to understand, the power balance may shift again. By giving more power to the human (employee), trust may be achieved.

Of course, I hasten to mention that this task of promoting transparency is not getting easier. Technology is becoming more complex and can be applied to almost anything. It makes it more difficult to truly understand the internal workings of the machine. For this reason, it is a requirement that leaders today are tech-savvy enough to understand and explain, at least, the basic reasons why the algorithm has become a player in today's workforce.

3. Managing technology education

Humans are known to work together with others more easily if they have a shared sense of purpose. So, when algorithms enter the collaborative work circle as the new co-worker, an important job for any leader will be to explain the purpose that they serve. Leaders will need to know the answer to the simple question: why do we use algorithms in the first place?

The importance of addressing this question underscores the need for leaders in the 21st century to be reasonably tech savvy. Before you start sweating and pondering on whether you are tech savvy enough, let me assure you right away that it will not be the case that you need to know all the inner workings of an algorithm. As I mentioned earlier, there is no need for you to become a coder. What leaders do need to do is to stay abreast of the major trends in technology. This kind of awareness should be present to understand why it is that digital transformation processes are currently happening in the business world and whether your own company needs to do the same, and if so, in what way.

As leaders set out visions for the future of the company, they need to understand how the use of new technology can help develop strategies that help the competitiveness and long-term sustainability of the company. This type of leadership action in an era dominated by automation clearly requires leaders to be aware of the most recent technology trends. They also need to acquire sensitivities to the challenges that the introduction of algorithms brings to a human work force.

These sensitivities can be very well trained and maintained by, for example, being involved personally in the recruitment process of data scientists and engineers, and the introduction of these new recruits to their business colleagues in other departments. In fact, in the company of tomorrow, collaboration between teams of data scientists and teams in the other business areas (sales, marketing, finance, HR and so forth) will be needed more than ever, in order to create more effective solutions to future challenges.

Continuous education

Companies thus need to prepare their leaders to think in ways that combine their business knowledge and expertise with a greater awareness of the opportunities and challenges that technology brings. This requirement to familiarize yourself with recent technological developments is linked closely with today's global mission of lifelong learning. Governments and companies alike have embraced the idea that their citizens and workforces need to be better prepared for a future where technology will bring many disruptions.

To meet these demands, training programs must be developed, and an attitude of learning continuously encouraged, at all levels of society. A report published by *MIT Sloan Management Review* and Deloitte shows that an increasing number of companies are investing significantly to achieve digital maturity in their workforce.[160] This is done by engaging in activities of continuous learning.

There is a good reason for this goal. Companies are shown to perform better and create more innovation when the cultural mindset is one of learning. Many companies consider it an important responsibility for leaders to educate and promote learning.[161] Of course, the best way to do this is to set an example, show leaders' enthusiasm for life-long learning.

Enthusiasm initiated at the top will cascade down and inspire others at lower levels in the organization. The first step for leaders is therefore to educate themselves about the technology employed within the company.

4. Managing employees' expectations

The fact that many employees distrust algorithms indicates that they have specific expectations on how an algorithm should function. These kinds of expectations may well be biased, thereby further complicating how humans and algorithms mingle. Research has demonstrated that humans tend to expect algorithms to deliver advice that is perfect.[162] In general, we expect any use of technology to be perfect. No mistake should be made or allowed once algorithms are brought into the workforce. And, if a mistake does take place, then trust in the automated advisor is lost immediately and completely.

Of course, we also do not like our human co-workers to make mistakes, but, contrary to when algorithms make mistakes, trust is not lost right away. The reason for this is that we know that as humans we are not perfect. And, because we are not perfect, we are able to forgive other humans and maintain trust to some extent. Algorithms, on the other hand, are supposed to be perfect, so why should we forgive them?

And, here lies the danger. If forgiveness cannot be granted, conflicts will build and create a non-co-operative work environment between humans and algorithms. In addition, because humans do not have much experience in dealing with algorithms as part of the work context, they are not yet at ease when working with them. Our biases and stereotypical expectations will then have a major impact on how we behave towards them.

One solution that could help is the *contact* hypothesis. According to this hypothesis, the longer that humans work together with algorithms, the more comfortable they will feel in this specific relationship. Consequently, the advice of algorithms will gradually be taken more seriously and, hence, used more often.

5. Learning to explain the how and why

It should be clear by now that when employees lack an explanation for what algorithms do and why they do it, trust will suffer. It is not only the trust in algorithms that will decline, but also trust in the company. In particular, companies that decide to make use of algorithms without making sense of them to their employees will be trusted less. As such, it is no luxury but a requirement that leaders explain clearly the value and operation mode of algorithms to their employees. With better explanations and more transparency, we can expect less resistance from employees towards algorithms. This will pave the way to more integrative and fruitful collaborations between humans and algorithms.

Interestingly, this issue of explaining the use of technology has not gone unnoticed and is surfacing everywhere in business. For example, Jack Dorsey, CEO of Twitter, noted, "We need to do a much better job at explaining how our algorithms work. Ideally opening them up so that people can actually see how they work. This is not easy for anyone to do."

So, how to deliver the best and most adequate explanation? The Merriam-Webster dictionary defines an explanation as "the act or process of telling, showing," or "being the reason for or cause of something." Explanations are thus meant to provide meaning, justification and transparency about why something is needed or available.[163] And, with explanation comes common understanding, more trust and co-operation, and less conflict.[164]

How to explain?

To achieve these positive outcomes, explanations need to include a few features. First, explanations need to be perceived as sincere.[165] An explanation is sincere when you are seen as being an honest and authentic person. Such an impression shows that you feel personally involved in making sure everyone knows what is going on. Coming across as authentic lets people know you will take their issue seriously.

When it concerns humans, we like to see people who are able to explain their actions and decisions. There should be no need to ask for someone else to explain the decisions you made. However, this is not the case for algorithms. Even if an algorithm were able to explain its actions, it would still be limited in impact, simply because it does not have an authentic sense of intelligence.

Second, explanations need to record legitimate reasons for the situation that has occurred.[166] It needs to make clear that logical and fair reasons exist for why certain decisions and actions have been undertaken. In a sense, almost anything can be explained, but if the explanation is perceived to be not fair or illegitimate, it may backfire. Finally, explanations need to provide adequate reasons for why the situation needs to be like this.[167] The reasons need to be high-quality, easy to verify and come across as believable. This is more easily achieved if your reasons are backed up by empirical evidence and illustrated by examples.

Leadership empowers algorithms

Algorithms will be part of the team. Leaders are expected to guide teams in this transformative process, which means that leaders in the age of automation must learn to not only empower humans, but algorithms too. In this way, the right circumstances need to be created so that algorithms can fulfil their full potential and help reveal new business opportunities and value.

Which abilities do leaders need to show to achieve this kind of empowerment?

Table 2: The empowering abilities for algorithms by the leaders of tomorrow

Empowerment abilities	Actions taken
Delegating work to the algorithm	Give autonomy in task execution Accept full responsibility Create a loop of feedback meetings
Identify which data are most important	Set priorities Use purpose to select the right dataset
Use the right frame to ask questions	Use purpose to frame the right questions for each business area

1. **Delegating work to the algorithm**

The first important task for leaders is to put the algorithm to work: algorithms need to be given jobs to do. They need to be put into the work circle and placed in charge of a specific number of tasks. Only then can an algorithm truly become a co-worker.

However, there is more to the task than simply having the algorithm analyze data that you have selected. An algorithm also delivers output and this output will determine future steps to be taken. Can algorithms take these steps?

Yes, they can – at least in the context of the simpler tasks. It is fair to say that algorithms will only become more sophisticated over time. This means that, at some point in the future, algorithms will be ready to be given the autonomy to determine and execute their own decisions. This is the moment when (simple) tasks will become fully automated. Interestingly, this scenario depicts a reality in which leaders have to empower both algorithms and humans.

How do leaders empower humans?

Humans feel most motivated when they experience a sense of autonomy in the tasks they conduct. This can be empowering for employees because they can decide on how to use their abilities to produce the best possible outcome. Through learning from and mastering tasks, employees grow into their job. Such processes allow them to tackle more difficult and complex problems in the future. In a somewhat similar vein, in the near future, algorithms will also have to be given a certain sense of autonomy.

What we expect from algorithms is that they work fast, produce accurate numbers and identify trends, that, if simple enough, can be applied immediately. Knowing this, leaders then need to decide which tasks and in what way to delegate work to an algorithm. Delegating work to algorithms frees up the time and work schedule of other employees, who can then focus on more complicated tasks. At the same time, it also allows for implementing the algorithm in the most optimal way possible. After all, if organizations invest significantly in their automation efforts, then it would be a waste of money if the algorithm cannot be trusted to fulfil their role.

In theory, this all sounds fine, but we do need to be cognizant of a limitation that algorithms carry with them into the work context. This limitation concerns the fact that they are usually developed in settings where no co-creation with humans is investigated *a priori*. Algorithms have not been tested beforehand in how to function and optimize their value in a social context.

Therefore, algorithms do not possess an intuitive sense of working together with a human. Leaders will need to experiment in how to best integrate an algorithm in a social context. Leaders will also have to be sensitive about how to communicate that certain tasks are to be delegated to an algorithmic co-worker, because the mere fact of delegation in this case will mean that the algorithm will work autonomously. This process has two sides.

The art of delegation

First of all, leaders will have to decide *when* to tell human employees that they have to defer to algorithmic judgment. This is not an easy task! Indeed, humans will usually resist such delegation efforts and may even resort to strategies of sabotage. In this context, the right kind of explanation is needed, where the leader expresses deep sympathy for the human employee and the impact on his/her work experience. At the same time, the leader needs to explain why it is necessary that the human employee complies with the advice delivered by an algorithm.

Put simply, the first side of the delegation process requires that a leader creates the room needed for the algorithm to perform well, while at the same time also taking full responsibility for the decision to have algorithms and humans work together in co-creation. Responsibility here means that the leader is liable for the outcomes that the algorithm reveals, in both its autonomous and collaborative tasks. As the leader, you should be willing to correct the work situation if those outcomes prove unsatisfactory.

How can leaders determine whether work outcomes are unsatisfactory in the collaborative context between algorithms and humans? With this question, we touch upon the second side of the delegation process. Even though leaders can grant more autonomy to algorithms, boundaries regarding their execution power need to be drawn. The goal of delegating tasks to algorithms is not to replace human employees, but to augment their abilities. Therefore, as in any delegation process, feedback meetings are needed to continuously evaluate the performance of the algorithm. Based on these meetings, boundaries to what an algorithm can do will be negotiated, set and re-set.

This feedback will have to be given by the peers of the algorithm, which, in the case of an algorithm, will be the human employee. The human employee is the end user of the algorithm here and therefore a source of feedback. An important point to stress here is that the input from the human employee in evaluating the algorithm needs to be tested on the earlier mentioned biases as well. As such, leaders need to build new work cultures in which biases and distrust are reduced as much as possible to assure that giving feedback will not be seen by employees as an opportunity to simply oppose the algorithm.

2. **Identify which data is most important**

Algorithms can make external data transparent so that we can more easily identify significant trends to help optimize business processes and value created. However, an algorithm cannot achieve any of this if it is not fed with data. So, who decides what kind of data is given to the algorithm?

These are important questions because intelligent machines will produce better insights and identify more useful trends if the data is of high quality. If the data quality is poor, one cannot expect optimal use of algorithms. In fact, when using low quality data, algorithms will underperform and may even perform worse than humans. As a result, they will face serious opposition from their co-workers and investments the company made in automation may quickly become futile. This possibility is a scenario that many companies take seriously, but nevertheless have difficulties in solving.

What is interesting to observe is that in cases where the algorithm fails because of poor data quality, organizational leadership does not so much blame themselves and their own costly investments, but rather the human workforce. In my consultancy efforts, I hear such comments very often. When things go wrong, blame the humans!

If such accusations are made, it is easy to understand that organizations could then be tempted to think that it might be easier to get rid of the human employee rather than the automated one. But, of course, we all know by now that it is not that simple. A more obvious explanation lies in the fact that too little guidance and clarity has been provided, to both humans and algorithms, in what needs to be achieved. In other words, if the organization is not clear about its purpose and the goals that come along with it, it will be difficult to identify the kind of data that needs to be used as input to the automated workforce.

Purpose makes for data

If it is unclear and not well-defined what kind of data needs to be used, the resulting outcome from any algorithmic effort will be so much less useful to the pursuit of company goals. Dewhurst and Willmot (2014) call this failure of algorithms acting in optimal ways, the "garbage in/garbage out" principle.[168] If algorithms have to assist in making decisions and the appropriate data is not employed, why should we then expect that business processes and outcomes will become optimized? Algorithms cannot address the quality of data issue, so it is up to leaders to make those choices. Leaders set the priorities and those priorities will guide the collection of high-quality data. This reality also requires leaders to be clear about and embrace the purpose of the organization they are leading.

Decision making is key to effective leadership and this is no different in the age of automation.[169] Leaders of tomorrow will still have to make strategic decisions, use soft skills in dealing with employees, and decide on the opportunities on offer for all stakeholders. The one big difference, however, is that in the future, algorithms will have to be included in the decision-making process. One important consequence of this change is that leaders will more than ever need to consider the importance of data quality for the value they want to create. Rather than processing and analysing the massive amounts of data available, leaders need to decide to focus on which type of data is required and for what reason.

Leaders today should be trained to recognize the purpose of the company and translate this knowledge into asking the right kinds of question. Organizations and their leadership need to envision the kind of business situation they want to grow into. They have a specific reason for pursuing that vision, and this is their purpose. The *why* of their business.

Purpose, as such, provides meaning to the vision a leader articulates. And, if we let our purpose dictate the goals we strive for and the actions we undertake, we are on the path to achieving value for the various stakeholders. From this point of view, it is clear that a purpose-driven approach to data selection is needed if we want to optimize the use of algorithms in decision making.

3. **Use the right framework to ask questions.**

Purpose helps to identify the priorities of a company, which will then direct the selection process of data for analysis. As such, purpose provides a framework that can be used to look at the external reality (data). The benefit of a framework is that it can also help in guiding the specific questions that need to be answered. Frameworks help color the kind of questions you need to ask to promote the development of innovative solutions. Asking the right kind of questions also helps to ensure that we continue to make the best use of the highest quality data.

A focus on purpose helps to select data regarding each stakeholder (customer, employee, supplier, shareholder and so forth) involved. But, of course, not every business department (marketing, sales, HR, finance, operations and so forth) is required to solve the same problems. It is therefore important that leaders use the purpose-driven framework to infer the type of questions that should be asked in each business department.

CHAPTER 8
Co-Creation as a New Beginning?

M UCH WORK IN organizations today is done in teams. In an interconnected world, it is not a surprise that people often work together in virtual groups to achieve goals they cannot achieve alone. Teamwork is instrumental to achieving innovative solutions within complex environments. Teams are better able to bring a diversity of ideas to the table, respond quicker to complex challenges, and allocate ownership for tasks to multiple people at the same time. Deloitte has even suggested that in today's digital world, organizations increasingly structure their work setting as being based on a *network of teams*.[170]

Even though volatile team dynamics are crucial for delivering fast and innovative solutions, it is also necessary for each team member to have a list of tasks they need to complete. Such tasks, which must have clearly defined criteria, can then be used to decide what kind of person is needed on the team. Today, teams require fast and transparent knowledge analysis, and therefore a new kind of member is entering the team. This new team member is not human, but algorithmic in nature.

Iron Man as the example to follow?

Inspired by the character J.A.R.V.I.S. (just a very intelligent system) in the movie *Iron Man*, we strive to build teams that rely on co-creation between humans and algorithms. We need to combine our strengths to cope with future challenges. A variety of tasks will thus be executed by either a human or an algorithm, but the most important goal will be to ensure that the efforts of both types of members can be integrated to create the required added value. For this effort to succeed, we need leaders to co-ordinate the efforts of humans and algorithms in ways that create something new. If humans and algorithms both represent a figure of one, then leaders need to ensure that their added value is a three. To achieve this, a leader's task will be two-fold.

First, as discussed in chapter seven, leaders need to empower humans and algorithms in their own specific ways. Algorithms will conduct tasks that require the skill of analyzing enormous volumes of data to optimize strategy. Machine intelligence makes existing data more transparent so that it can be used to make faster and more effective decisions. Humans will be used in sense-making tasks where perception, ethical judgment, intuition, empathy, and creative thinking is necessary. These so-called soft skills are especially needed in team efforts as they help to tacitly co-ordinate work relationships.

Second, leaders will have to ensure that the dynamics of a team composed of humans and algorithms are properly managed. In other words, leaders will now have to manage the *new diversity*. I refer to new diversity as today's reality, where algorithms will become the new teammates of human employees. As a consequence, teams will become more diverse, in terms of the skills on offer, but also in how the work will be done. Such a reality brings forward new challenges for leaders, the most important of which is being to understand what it is that can make interactions between humans and machines tick.

Leaders will be forced to think more deeply about how to make these new diversity team settings more effective than teams solely composed of human members. Companies that best manage the collaboration between humans and algorithms will be the ones that will be most successful in the future. And, be warned, it is not simply being able to promote the individual performance of the human member and the individual algorithm. No, it will depend on how well organizations can put the performance of both humans and algorithms together to create a mix that delivers something new.

This requirement makes clear that leaders in the future will be more responsible than ever for the success of their organization. They need to be able to tap into both their business and technological knowledge and use it to bring people and technology together. They will have to be intelligent in promoting co-creation between humans and algorithms. Mastering the ability of empowerment, as outlined in chapter seven, will be crucial. The ideal view on what I call empowering the new diversity is to ensure that both humans and algorithms achieve a collaborative relationship. The act of co-operation is understood as an effort in which members of a team, organization or society work together to achieve a common goal. It is a known fact that the human species survives not because of fighting with each other, but because of co-operation.

Co-operating in the new diversity

The same is likely to be true in today's era of automation. Co-operation, rather than competition, between humans and machines will bring the most benefits to all. A nice example of successful co-operation between humans and technology is demonstrated in the case of Hyundai Motors.[171] Hyundai is a Korean car manufacturer who employ many line workers. The work is tough and requires significant physical effort, which can lead to injuries and both physical and mental exhaustion. One of the strains of the job is that these workers have to do a lot of heavy lifting. Adopting the perspective that humans and machines can co-create, Hyundai has created exoskeletons – wearable robotics – that the line workers can use. The robotics developed allow workers to be more productive, while at the same time doing a better job in safeguarding their health.

What successful co-operation between humans and machines does is augment the abilities of individuals and teams. We talk about augmenting human abilities because the potential level of achievement due to the new diversity is higher than can be expected in teams composed only of humans. Another case that demonstrates how technology can augment human productivity can be found in the online company Stitch Fix in the US. Their algorithm-driven business model helps human employees to provide personalized styling service to customers. Data (preferences, body measures and budget) are provided by customers and analyzed by algorithms, which then provide recommendations. If a customer follows up these recommendations and adds further preferences to their profiles, algorithms make suggestions for future purchases. Using algorithms in this way makes for more effective salespeople and happier, more satisfied customers.

Within team settings, algorithms can also augment the processes that create output. Indeed, intelligent systems can be used to augment decision making which, in turn, can lead to better actions. An example which illustrates this is algorithms being used to help doctors make diagnoses, a practice that enabled doctors to deliver higher-quality individualized treatments. Algorithms can access individual profiles, analyze that data and find patterns across patient populations. This refined knowledge, combined with the human skills of intuition, empathy, and creativity, will make for better outcomes. For example, when examining how to increase cancer detection in the images of lymph node cells, it was shown that an algorithm-only approach had a 7.5% error rate, while a human-only approach had a 3.5% error rate. The combined approach, however, revealed an error rate of only 0.5%.[172]

To be an orchestral conductor

Like any team effort, co-operation between parties needs to be properly co-ordinated. And, this is where leaders in the future will earn their rewards. In the 21st century, one of the most important leadership abilities will be to act as an orchestral conductor, to have humans and algorithms working together in symphony. Acting as an orchestral conductor could even be taken literally, as demonstrated by the Chinese telecom giant, Huawei, who in 2018 explored whether this *new diversity* style of collaboration could employ AI-technology to complete Schubert's Symphony No.8, originally started in 1822.[173] The first two movements of the symphony were completed by the master himself, but the last two, for unknown reasons, were never completed.

To undertake the task, the company utilized the AI technology of the Huawei Mate 20 Pro smartphone. After having the technology study 90 compositions written by Schubert, Huawei's AI technology translated them into code and worked to extend them. The AI also listened to the first two movements of Schubert's Symphony No. 8 to analyze the key musical elements. The technology then combined its analysis with the knowledge acquired from Schubert's pieces to end up with a new melody for the third and fourth movement.

The one-million-dollar question, of course, is whether the AI was able to decide which new combination best represented the emotions and atmosphere that Schubert wanted his music pieces to communicate. The obvious problem in this project is that AI cannot feel, nor is it possible for machines to understand the soul of an artist. The *new diversity* idea implies that at this point humans have to enter the work equation. The human employee asked to lead this specific project was the composer Lucas Cantor – who writes for DreamWorks Animation and is known for many movie music pieces. His primary task was to avoid the awful fate that the ending to Schubert's Symphony No. 8 would sound like elevator music.

So, what did we learn from this experiment? The most interesting finding was that Cantor himself was very positive about the collaboration and compared it to actually working with another composer. So, the work experience from the human side seemed to be acceptable, even *enjoyable*. According to Cantor, one reason for this was because the AI composer had no ego, something that he would usually have had to consider when making changes to a human composer's work. The AI-driven composer was never in a bad mood and never protested when Cantor sent back pieces with a request to re-work. Also important was the fact that, because of the work process and the incredible pace of AI itself, the 18-minute piece was written in just a few exchanges. Overall, efficiency went up, the work process seemed enjoyable and the end product was rated as *good* by a critical human audience.

This example helps us to understand what a leader will have to do when empowering the new diversity to drive better performance. As Venema recently noted: "One weakness remains apparent: algorithms are poor at interacting with humans in scenarios where subtle forms of co-operation are required."[174] Indeed, algorithms learn and generate knowledge by relying on observations and identifying data patterns, but do not think at deeper levels of intelligence, where emotions and empathy are at work. For this reason, guidance by humans is key when making decisions that involve common sense and awareness of the strategic, moral and social dynamics that are at play in organizational decision-making. As Bernie Meyerson, IBM's chief innovation officer, said: "Humans bring common sense to the work; by its definition, common sense is not a fact-based undertaking. It is a judgment call."[175]

Initiating co-operation

In light of the reality that algorithms innately lack common sense, it is crucial that they are used in the right way. And this way has to be decided by the team leader. At the same time, humans, with their own unique capabilities, will have to be used in ways that are best matched with their profile and skill set. A first task for a leader is therefore one that involves *task allocation*. Leaders need to shape team structures by deciding which tasks are allocated to algorithms and which ones to humans. But this is not where it stops. One benefit of teamwork is that different ideas can be collected and provide more integrative solutions to problems.

As the Huawei example shows, a challenge for leaders will be to motivate human employees to make use of the information that algorithms provide to the team. As such, leaders will initially have to motivate human team members to *accept* algorithms as co-workers. Then, human employees need to go beyond acceptance to perceive and value algorithms as *useful* team members. Such a changed perception can only be achieved if leaders empower human employees to initiate interactions with algorithms.

Algorithms do not possess the qualities to initiate co-operative relationships, however, they can be included as a more active member once relationships have been established. In order to achieve integrative solutions, humans must be motivated to take the first step. Leaders therefore will have to empower human employees to take a more *active* role in their relationships with algorithms at work. The best way to inspire such active commitment is to ensure first of all that employees are knowledgeable enough about the intelligent technology with which they are supposed to work. This will require leaders to make their employees more tech-savvy, which, as we have seen in chapter seven, is labelled under *continuous education*.

Understanding the need for algorithms can empower humans to be more willing to use the input generated by those same algorithms. Therefore, in addition to the leader's responsibility to make human employees accept algorithms as team members, they will also have to structure the work setting in such a way that the output generated by both algorithms and human agents is collected and made transparent to all. This requires leadership to aggregate the output of humans and algorithms into a collective decision. To achieve this, leaders will have to act as a kind of *transactive memory*, in which they serve as the binding glue between the different agents in the team. From this position, leaders must make all knowledge available, foster integration as supervised by human employees and ultimately decide on its use to achieve the goals of the team and company.[176]

Creating added value

All these requirements for the leaders of tomorrow center around the skill of promoting co-operation between humans and machines. As all our examples demonstrate, such outcomes can only be achieved if the value that is created by algorithms can be translated to the human context, where it can create value relevant to human *end-users*. As Dewhurst and Willmot (2014, p. 2) argue, "the contextualization of small-scale, machine-made decisions is likely to become an important component of tomorrow's leadership tool kit."[177]

One specific area where this co-operative ability can impact almost immediately is in the working of HR departments, which are important for recruiting the right kind of employees. Algorithms can provide many benefits in this process; they can be used to analyze the massive amounts of data collected over years to identify suitable candidates, or even to focus on the right kind of information in a recruitment session. For example, Jobaline, a job-placement site, uses intelligent voice-analysis algorithms to evaluate job applicants. The algorithm assesses paralinguistic elements of speech, such as tone and inflection, predicts which emotions a specific voice will elicit, and identifies the type of work at which an applicant will likely excel.

Finally, once the right kind of people are working in the organization, you want to keep them. A study from the National Bureau of Economic Research demonstrated that low-skill, service sector workers (where retention rates are low) stayed in the job 15% longer when an algorithm was used to judge their employability.[178]

Once the appropriate work setting is created, co-operation will be facilitated, but another important question remains. What to do once co-operation is achieved? Traditional business models assume that team outcomes will directly contribute to the goals and vision of the company. Leaders therefore need to know the key priorities to pursue and how to ensure that integrative solutions directly contribute to the pursuit of company goals. This will have to be achieved by communicating clearly to employees the reasons why they have to perform certain tasks alongside the ultimate goal.

At the same time, leaders need to be able to communicate with data scientists to ensure that the right priorities are used when calculation principles are coded for algorithms. These responsibilities underscore the importance for leaders to be able to connect with employees with different professional backgrounds, ensure that those employees use algorithms in efficient ways, and that value is created by co-creation between humans and algorithms.

A final question to address is what happens to the leader when priorities are known and co-operation is facilitated? If leaders have installed these processes, do they remain participative?

Indeed, if this point is arrived at, the leader should participate less and devote more attention to strategic thinking and development. A famous saying is that leadership is about making others perform better, so that they have to do less. When I mention this quote in my classes, many students' express interest, but not necessarily for the right reasons. They are mainly attracted to the prospect of doing less!

This kind of interpretation always forces me to make clear that doing less in this context does not mean the same as doing nothing. On the contrary, it means that once your team knows what to do, and they have been empowered in the best ways possible, it is time for leaders to step back and devote their time to the more traditional tasks of leadership. This includes planning and developing the important strategic steps a company needs to take in the future to ensure its competitiveness and long-term sustainability.

CHAPTER 9
The Art of Leadership: Purpose and Inclusion

THE CURRENCY THAT makes organizations run and survive over time is leadership. And with the introduction of rapidly changing technologies, this may be more important than ever before.

Today, a new currency has surfaced that increases the level of organizational success; its name: data. No, not the character Data from Star Trek, but actual data, gathered to help us understand what is happening in the world. Data is now considered by many as one of the most valuable resources that organizations have at their disposal. So, it is important for leadership today to deal with massive amounts of data and to integrate the insights derived from data analysis into decision making. With this reality in sight, algorithms are increasingly penetrating organizations and forcing us to think about their impact on how we run our organizations.

One very specific challenge concerns the extent to which algorithms will become autonomous decision makers in our organizations. It is a challenge because it brings with it the risk that humans gradually become more dependent on the abilities and advice offered by algorithms. If we become too dependent, we may end up being led by algorithms rather than us leading them. But, would we ever consider those algorithms as likely candidates to lead our organizations?

Well, consider the following. Algorithms are consistent learners, enabling them to enlarge their cognitive abilities with every new insight. The abilities that algorithms gain in this way are largely in the areas of speed of data processing, pattern recognition, and creating more transparency in the data available. These are all areas that can make organizations smarter and help them make more accurate forecasts and predictions. Hence, it could make sense to have algorithms develop into leaders. But, as we have seen, the reality is that algorithms as leaders is not an easy sell and unlikely to happen.

Know your context

One thing that algorithms are less likely to learn and develop is a kind of human-like intuition that recognizes the impact of changing contexts. This limitation makes them *de facto* unfit to lead any organization.

Why does context recognition matter?

We know that algorithms today are so sophisticated that they can beat humans in almost any game. Since 1997, when world champion Gary Kasparov was beaten by Deep Blue in a game of chess, technology has improved so much that today even the AI in our cell phones could beat many world champions. But, and here it comes, they can only do so in the specific context of that *one* game – not in any other game. The reason for this is that, in reality, an algorithm does not even know that it is playing a game. Algorithms do so well in playing games simply because they are better than a human at analyzing and identifying successful behavioral patterns and employing them to win.

So, if it is the case that an algorithm does not know what a game is, how then can we expect an algorithm to be able to lead others?

Algorithms will very likely not understand the wide range of abilities that leaders use across situations to be successful. In fact, algorithms are, for example, limited in seeing the relevance of showing empathy when employees get stressed or when situations have changed in such a way that employees feel somewhat at a loss. Because of their analytical strengths, algorithms are applicable to anything related to management, but their weakness with soft skills makes them less suited for leadership. Leadership is a different kind of animal, something that algorithms cannot easily translate.

As we have seen in chapter six, it is the soft skills that make us uniquely human and the most likely candidates to lead. This is all great, but another question we also need to address is what kind of leadership styles make the best use of our human abilities?

This question is important because it will be exactly those leadership styles that our future leaders will have to display in an increasingly automated work environment. Below, I will explain that there are two leadership styles, purpose-driven and inclusive, which will be prominent in the future.

On the importance of purpose

For an automated workforce to work effectively it requires access to data. Data is oil for algorithms to create value for the organization. Although data is often hailed as a new kind of resource for today's organizations, the reality is that data has always been important to business!

It is only the case that today – with an increased focus on the notion of big data – we are so much more eager to work with data to the benefit of our organization. Since their inception, business schools have taught that one of the first and most important steps towards starting a business is to ensure that you analyze the data out there. In fact, businesspeople have always known that it is necessary to become familiar with data that can reveal what customers want, what opportunities exist, which industries have significant growth margins and so forth.

With the arrival of digital data, we have entered an era where the ability to work with data has become something of a highly valued expertise. Today, organizations have so much data available that finding out which data is important and which one not has become a (valued) skill in itself. Organizations today need to be more equipped than ever to structure their data efficiently and make it accessible across different systems and departments. The necessity for such a co-ordinated approach makes clear that organizations need leadership that is able to interpret available data in light of the company's goals. Today, leaders need to use data in ways that optimize their business strategies. Isn't this happening then? If we listen to the markets, it seems like that is not the case. Organizations in fact are failing largely in structuring their data and building a data-focused culture.[179]

A problem thus seems to be that organizations today are failing to build a culture that structures and utilizes the massive amounts of data available. As companies are often unable to build the right culture that meets the demands of a data-driven business environment, we can then only conclude that the right kind of leadership is not present. So, what kind of leadership is needed to ensure that we achieve the best outcomes in a business environment that runs on data?

LEADERSHIP BY ALGORITHM

To answer this question, allow me to ask another question first. Specifically, why is it that, as an organization, we need to use data?

We use data to develop business models that will help us design the right strategies to create value. A business model describes how we want to do business; which stakeholders' interests matter; and identifies the actions that we need to take. Business models thus need data and we cannot do without. But, of course, we do not need just any kind of data. We need data that can help us to decide on strategies that create the kind of value that we, as an organization, care about. The kind of value organizations care about is defined by the purpose an organization. Purpose makes clear why we are in business in the first place and, as such, should be non-negotiable. It is therefore supposed to direct and guide the efforts of a company.

The notion of purpose has gained a lot of traction in the last few years. When companies enter a new, complex situation and realize that change is needed, organizations ideally should fall back on their purpose to guide strategic decisions. Leaders are important in this process because they need to help us to focus on the things that matter most to the organization. In an era where data significantly shapes our strategies, it is important to ensure that we use the right kind of data – right in the sense that they are relevant to the purpose we are pursuing. Organizations today cannot afford to be ambiguous about their purpose. Once the purpose is clear and shared by all, organizations are more efficient in using data to develop better business models. Purpose helps us to focus on the priorities and thus make it easier to select the most relevant data to work with.

Because of these challenges it is clear that the organization of tomorrow needs to be run by purpose-driven leaders. Purpose-driven leadership serves as a compass, guiding the company in its growth and delivery of success. Purpose-driven leadership consists of two important dimensions that can be developed and trained (see figure 2).

First of all, purpose provides the content to the *vision* of the organization.[180] When you are clear about your purpose, it will be easier to envision what you want to achieve. Second, a clear purpose helps to establish the values that you want to pursue and how you will display this in both life and work. It is important that others understand your values, so that they can understand how you do business, treat others, and, more specifically, what you consider *ethical*.

[*114*]

Figure 2: Being purpose-driven by being a visionary and ethical leader

Visionary leadership

When work environments are transformed into settings where human employees interact with algorithms, people may become worried about losing their jobs; concerned about the longer-term implications of automation for the organization; and lack the confidence to use advice provided by algorithms. It is in moments like this that leadership is required, as the integration of algorithms in the decision-making cycle needs to make sense to people to be effective. To achieve such sense of meaning, leaders are required to communicate their vision in a way that justifies the use of algorithms as co-workers. The vision should depict what the future may look like if we embark on this new journey.

In the automated era, this new journey is characterized by a situation where humans and algorithms collaborate to co-create. However, to achieve this kind of collaboration, employees need to be inspired and empowered, which is something visionary leaders do.[181] A visionary leader energizes people by building a bridge between what we see happening today and what we should do with it to ensure value is created in the future.

Communication of a vision can thus help people to link present efforts with what can possibly be achieved in the future.[182] At the same time, this transformational process signals what really matters to the organization and its members. Indeed, the added value created by bridging the present and the future has to be appealing to employees so that they commit to the journey of change.[183]

How to develop your visionary abilities?

A vision is needed that inspires people to follow your chosen direction by contributing significant time and effort to their jobs. After all, it is the contributions of the others that will make your leadership effective. In the era of automation, leaders are only effective if the vision of algorithms and humans working together is supported by employees. What do leaders need to focus on to promote their visionary skills?

- **Be aware of the value you want to create**
As the articulation of a vision implies a change in the current situation, leaders need to train themselves to be clear on what kind of value they wish to create for both themselves and others. The direction that you choose therefore needs to make sense in light of your values.

To highlight such value, you should stay motivated and energetic. Indeed, being resilient is one of the biggest challenges for a leader driving change. So, it is important that you take good care of your health and well-being and, above all, keep nurturing the values that give purpose to what you do.

The direction taken by your vision needs to make sense to others. As such, communicate clearly what is waiting ahead and why it is so important that the desired outcome be achieved. The vision should be formulated in such a way that everyone also realizes that they need to participate to succeed. It is also crucial that employees understand that your vision, which incorporates algorithms as co-workers, is happening to foster a better performing organization.

Obviously, being ready to deal with the demanding task of developing and communicating an appealing vision requires you to do your homework.

One thing that successful visionary leaders do is engage in scenario planning exercises. In these exercises, you imagine the different ways a vision can be communicated and explore which version is likely to be the most effective way to help your audience connect with the tasks that you are asking of them (i.e. working with the new diversity).

- **Be courageous in setting the stage**

A vision holds the promise of a road map that will help create value, but also challenge the old ways of working. This requires leaders to speak out in clear and direct ways, which may lead to people feeling pushed out of their comfort zones. Careful crafting of the message and preparation is thus needed. It is one thing to challenge people by pointing out what is wrong with the current situation. It is, however, another thing to persuade them to take your disruptive message seriously and consider you the legitimate authority to follow.

Courage takes two forms here and, in both, you will need to lead by example. First, you need to be courageous to challenge what people are used to and initiate change. Second, you need to show courage by putting in a continuous effort to make your vision a reality. Obviously these steps will be easier to take if your vision is one that you care deeply about. Rather than taking energy, these efforts will be meaningful to you and thus energize you.

- **Communicate to create**

Getting people to engage with your vision depends entirely on your ability to communicate. First, in your communication you should use the right context to explain to others *why* change is needed. Providing this context on the challenges that lie ahead will also help to explain why your vision can create the much-needed future value. For these reasons, it is advised that the kind of language used directs the audience to the most relevant and applicable data available. This data should highlight what is happening in our environment; what this means for our company (values); what this entails for our future (vision); and what our resources (the employees) need to do to drive this change.

In the context of automation, leaders should frame responses to say that the business requires algorithms to be utilized as the necessary platform to achieve the company's required values. If they do not, it is likely that algorithms will be seen as a threat, rather than an opportunity. Also, in your efforts to promote the idea of this new diversity as the new reality, your language should emphasize *we* rather than *them*. As I mentioned in chapter one, at this moment, humans and algorithms have not really moved far beyond interacting in terms of *us* versus *them*. To go beyond this kind of thinking, a vision needs to include the idea that we will only achieve value together.

Ethical leadership

Leadership that is pursuing a purpose is motivated by clearly defined values. Hence, purpose-driven leaders are ethically aware and able to make sound moral judgments and decisions. Leaders demonstrating the abilities of an ethical person inspire employees' motivation and commitment. When comparing someone you believe to be an ethical person with someone you do not, ask yourself: who would you rather follow?

I think the answer will be obvious to most of you. Ethical leaders are more influential because we perceive them to be high in integrity and can be relied upon to accept responsibility when needed. Since we hold these leaders in such high esteem, we use them as our models to engage in more responsible behavior ourselves.

It is exactly this kind of influence that algorithms cannot bring to the table. Algorithms do not have the ability to connect with humans at the level of shared values and desires. They cannot embody the ethical values that humans recognize in an (emotional) inspiring way. Put simply, algorithms cannot *lead by example* and thus cannot elicit an ethical mindset in others. It is exactly this ability to lead by example that is one of the key dimensions of ethical leadership. Ethical leaders serve as role models with the aim of providing ethical guidance to employees.[184] It is through the virtuous actions of leaders that followers are educated and motivated in ethical ways!

Reducing the complexity of ethics

So, does all of the above mean that algorithms are completely excluded from the business of leading in ethical ways? Not necessarily. Some ethical principles (as based on the philosophy of Immanuel Kant) assume a rational approach to what is the right thing to do. For example, Kant's idea of the categorical imperative states that people should be guided by fundamental ethical principles e.g. you should not lie. This principle should be used across all situations. Algorithms can definitely learn to make ethical judgments in such a way. This practice means that ethics will have to be seen as a set of universal principles that apply across all situations.

In such algorithmic reality, however, several risks exist. First, ethics will largely run in scripted ways and, as such, be experienced as fixed and robotic. If we accept this type of ethical decision making, we would adopt a leadership model that follows a reductionist approach, which cannot deal with the ethical complexities which occur in reality.

It would also simply be unfair. Each stakeholder has their own perspective on any given decision being made, and at least some sensitivity to these different perspectives should be considered by any leadership. Therefore, it is fair to say that when ethics are at stake, we need leaders who are aware of the different interests and concerns of the stakeholders involved. It is this ability to (emotionally) connect to the concerns and perspectives of others that makes ethical leaders so effective. It allows them to create psychologically safe workplaces where employees can speak up.

Ethical leadership cannot only be based on the application of rational decision models, it has to be built on an ability to show empathy, combined with the skill to accommodate the concerns of all people involved.

Augmenting ethics through automation

To bring our scope of ethical leadership in an automated era into focus, it is safe to say that ethical leadership cannot be replaced by algorithms. As explained in chapter six, one unique human ability is to make ethical judgments based on concerns of care and the ability to empathize. Without these unique characteristics, ethics become something mechanical and run the risk of ending up as another ticking-the-box exercise. I think that ethics deserve better treatment. Algorithms may, however, play a supporting role in arriving at judgments of what is right or wrong. It would mean that algorithms can also take the role of providing augmenting capability to leaders making ethical choices.

Business ethics scholars have introduced the distinction of ethical leaders being both *moral people* and *moral managers*.[185] As moral managers, ethical leaders are expected to comply with laws and regulations, establish ethical expectations and hold employees accountable. Such tasks correspond well with a more administrative approach. Indeed, laws and expectations can be verified in objective ways. As management by algorithm is a certainty waiting to happen, algorithms could well take care of the managerial dimension of ethical decision making.

It is a different story, however, when we refer to the need for ethical leaders to be moral *people*. It is this dimension that turns ethical leaders into effective and inspiring leaders, who motivate others to act in ethical ways. If our leaders are moral people, they will connect with us in more authentic ways. After all, seeing leaders as individuals caring about morals is likely to connect more deeply with employees than algorithms taking an ethical stand. As such, the ability to transfer ethical abilities cannot be grounded in an algorithmic ability to make a rational analysis of all the ethical principles out there.

How to develop your ethical leadership abilities?

Ethics matter in today's business world. The main ambition of any ethical leader is to ensure that a work culture is built where employees are ethically savvy enough to judge the right course of action. How to achieve such influence?

- **Be clear on your own values**

Your actions should be the best representative of your values. So, you need to walk the talk. In fact, the information that people have about your behavior is spontaneously categorized in people's brain as reflecting who you are as a person. Only then will people say whether you have a good or bad character.

As such, if you are not consistent and confident in how you want to treat others, those that are supposed to follow you will also be unclear on the issue. As a result, they will be unable to categorize you as a moral person and less likely to comply with the initiatives you develop. Therefore, it is imperative that leaders engage in reflective exercises that reveal what it is that drives you in life and work; what those drives mean in light of the values that you preach; and how you can derive energy from following and executing those values in your leadership role.

- **Do not only allow rules to dictate ethics**

It is no secret that people do not like to work in uncertain business settings. For this reason, we are quick to employ fixed rules that reduce uncertainty and ambiguity. For sure, rules do help to know how to act, but do they really inspire and motivate us to be the *best version* of ourselves? Probably not.

Why would this be the case? First, rules can indeed create a framework that helps to guide decisions on how to act. However, rules are usually reactive, which means that a rule is implemented after something went wrong. As such, using rules as your guiding moral compass is a rational way of acting and does not allow you to anticipate and understand instances where ethics lapse. You can only be reactive, not pro-active, when it comes down to ethics. It does not help to foster your intuitive sense of whether something is wrong or right. And, as such, you do not develop your ethical judgment.

Second, people are not predictably rational. In fact, they may be predictably irrational.[186] Rather than optimizing their behavioral strategies based on existing knowledge, human emotions disrupt logic and systematic processing of data in ways that makes them act differently than can be predicted by rational models.

These two points make it clear that if we consider a list of rules to be our ethical compass, and make sound ethical judgments based on these, then we are mistaken. It is not the case that rules cannot be used. No, it is the case that rules are not sufficient. And because they are not sufficient, they should not be treated as replacing – by means of algorithms – the ethical judgment of a human. Both are needed.

So, rules can be used to put together the ethics of the company, but not at the expense of preventing people from further developing their moral compass. As such, in addition to a clear set of rules, leaders have to discuss the standards and ethical expectations of the company they represent. This way, when ethical challenges – not mentioned or tackled by the set of rules – have to be dealt with, people will still have their ability to make sound judgment calls.

- **Create a culture of speaking up**

People will more easily engage in reflective thinking about the ethical consequences of business decisions, if the decision is perceived as fair by the workforce. To achieve such a level of engagement, employees need to be given a voice. Giving employees a say in how companies are run is not only effective from the perspective of enhancing performance, but also from the perspective of building ethical cultures.

Indeed, giving employees a voice contributes to an increase in trust and openness, which are crucial elements when building an ethical work culture. For example, companies where employees voice their concerns regarding questionable business practices have cultures where ethical awareness is high. The benefit of such increased awareness is that it helps to create a shared understanding of the values that the company considers a priority. It also helps to instill a culture in which ethical failures and lapses can be discussed and resolved as soon as possible.

Interestingly, contrary to making use of strongly regulated work environments (demanding rules to be obeyed) where monitoring systems require substantial financial investments, voice cultures are a cheap psychological way of motivating employees to be ethically aware.

- **Practice compassion**

It is a law of nature: people fail! True, not much debate is needed to establish that failure is a part of the human experience. Nevertheless, although failure may be part of who we are, we have a peculiar aversion towards our own and other's failure. There is nothing wrong with that, but what could be wrong is that this aversion motivates us to create systems (or even societies) aimed at rooting out failure altogether. Given our human nature, that is potentially a dangerous practice.

We know that to improve, one needs to be able to learn. So, how does learning take place? Learning happens when failure is still a possibility and conditions exist that allow time and effort to understand why failure happened. The same process takes place if we want our leaders to build a workforce that is ethically savvy. Indeed, if people fail and there is no human leadership in place to model ethical expectations, then it is safe to say that an ethically-aware work climate does not exist and people will not learn. To sharpen and develop ethical judgments, people need to understand why failure occurred in order to adjust their behaviour accordingly. Algorithms are not equipped to do this; they can neither build ethically-aware cultures by means of connecting to other employees, nor learn through a process of reflection over a span of time.

Summary: The benefits of purpose-driven leadership

Purpose-driven leadership is a requirement for businesses where automation is gradually increasing, because it allows for:

Setting priorities to look at data

Companies today are keen to combine different sources of data, like human resource data with social media data. This combination of more traditional data (available directly within the company) with online data reveals a massive volume of both structured and unstructured data. How do we look at such large volumes of data? Which data sets do we use to answer the questions we have? To make such choices, it is important that you, as a leader, know what kind of value you want to create. What is the purpose of the organization and what does it mean in terms of the value that we are creating for our different stakeholders? Having clear answers to these questions helps to frame the most relevant data.

Framing the right kind of questions for the right kind of strategy

Once the most relevant data is selected, we need to know what kind of questions we want to see answered. What is it that we want to ask the data?

Getting answers to the right questions will help to develop the right kind of strategy. The right set of questions helps identify the steps that need to be taken to achieve the purpose of the organization. The identification of these steps – as based on an accurate picture of your environment – thus feeds significantly into the strategy the company should adopt.

Providing a focus on how to analyze the data

Once questions are identified and initial analyzes are undertaken, new and unexpected challenges may emerge. In those moments, purpose serves as a guide to put these new challenges into the spotlight and potentially reconsider the data approaches used so far. Moments like this may reveal that data previously considered irrelevant may now be needed to delineate the most optimal strategy for the company. This observation again underscores the need for data to be widely shared within the company – access should not be restricted to data scientists. All departments should be able to access data, because new challenges will likely require a new pair of eyes to assess the problem. Under such circumstances, data scientists profit from the perspectives of other departments.

Helping to integrate new business demands with the values of the organization to create relevant and valuable strategies

Unstructured data can provide insights to trends that were not anticipated, or identify new demands that were not part of your original business model. According to analytics provider SAS, such new facts can directly drive the identification of strategies that will make the organization successful.

At the same time, unstructured data can also bring much uncertainty, for example, in how to look at the data. Such fact-driven decisions require a guiding framework, and this can be delivered by purpose-driven leadership. Indeed, when unstructured data enters the equation, leadership is needed to interpret how the data should be analyzed through the prism of corporate strategy, in order to create the required value to the organization.

Explaining clearly why data is collected and analyzed

The collection and analysis of data can be perceived as an intrusive act, and therefore regarded as violating the privacy of those whose data was collected. A real risk always exists that those stakeholders may consider data strategies to be a means of controlling them. It is therefore important that the reason for asking people for their personal data is always explained clearly, in light of the value the organization wants to create. If this is not done, data collection and analysis will be seen as an end in itself, rather than as a means to achieve something of greater value. It requires purpose-driven leadership to explain the goals of the data scientists and how their expertise will add to the value the organization wants to create. It will be the organizations that are able to create a shared purpose and use it to make sense of their data approach that will promote compliance most effectively.

On the importance of inclusive leadership

The introduction of algorithms to the human workforce will create a *new diversity* context. In this context, humans and machine will work together with the aim of augmenting human abilities to optimize the value that organizations can create. To achieve this outcome, it is essential that leadership can bring all the actors together in a spirit of collaboration.

Creating collaborative partnerships between humans and algorithms requires building an inclusive work setting. Achieving this requires leaders oriented towards the common good and motivated to use the potential of every team member to create the required added value. Inclusive leaders are thus not so concerned with exerting power and influence over others, but rather focused on creating a setting where everyone can participate in the collective effort required.[187]

Inclusive leaders facilitate work conditions that promote participation by all. Of course, to achieve such levels of participation requires leaders to show that they accept the new diversity idea and actively endorse it. It also requires leaders who can build a sense of connection between humans and algorithms.

As human skills need to be augmented by the use of algorithms, it is essential that the establishment of these connections are not driven by a mechanically-designed co-ordination script. Rather, inclusive leaders promote trust and respect towards humans and algorithms. The aim of inclusive leadership is to ensure that the workforce accepts such diversity in skills and motivates employees to integrate all perspectives to create new and valuable outcomes (see figure 3).

Figure 3: Being inclusive by connecting, being trustworthy, diversity-minded and humble

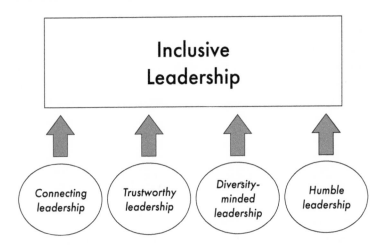

Connecting leadership

When are leaders effective? Does it depend on their individual performance? Or, does it depend on how they make others perform?

By now, it should be clear that it is more the latter than the former. Leadership is required to be the driving force of change. Successfully transforming a business requires that collective mobilization happens. Leaders are supposed to motivate and inspire people to walk in a certain direction. When this happens, change will take place. Leaders are therefore judged as effective if they can get the collective motivated.

Effective leaders therefore are the ones who can connect others. Leaders need to invest time, energy and resources into establishing high-quality relationships, but these investments will be reciprocated once connections are made. To find the right kind of connection, it is, first of all, important to know what drives people. What are their desires, what do they hope to achieve and why?

People more often connect if frequent and authentic communication takes place. Hence, a necessary skill for inclusive leaders is to be a good communicator, but also a good listener. Listening brings people together, rather than keeping them at a distance, and is therefore considered an essential part of inclusive leadership. Leaders who are able to bring people together and provide a sense of *togetherness*, use inclusive language emphasizing the connection between all members.[188] At this point you may ask, if we assume that inclusive leaders connect people, then isn't our assertion that their biggest strength should be to be quiet and simply listen a contradiction? Isn't that a passive approach?

I would beg to differ, and this is why.

To generate a connection between people, communication must establish a platform of common themes that bind people together. The advantage of a platform is that it makes information available to everyone and as soon as people start talking and communicating around a common theme, connection happens. But, before you can engage in this platform-building act, you need to do something else first. You need to find a theme or topic in which people have a shared interest. So, where do you get that information?

Right, from asking questions – and then being prepared to sit back and listen. Or, even more simply, just listening to what people are genuinely talking about. Listening is a more comprehensive behavior than most people think. It is an act that is not passive at all, since you are working to bring information together that can help highlight similarities between people and forge strong social connections.

Listening does not only identify what binds people together. Leaders who connect also need to mobilize people once they are brought together. And, in this stage of leadership, communication also matters. Once people are connected, leaders need to mobilize them to work together in line with a desired purpose. To do so, a clear message needs to be communicated that is contagious and inspires the collective to support the leader in their undertaking. This communicative aspect aligns closely with the ability to be visionary. Visionary leaders are known to use smart narratives, they are able to use the force of what connects people in their storytelling and subsequently uplift the collective to perform.

How to develop your connecting abilities

With the increasing need to share data, departments in organizations cannot work in silos anymore. Leaders who ensure data transparency across the organization therefore need to possess the skills to bring all these groups together and connect them in effective ways. Leaders with connecting skills:

- **Install a norm to listen first and talk second**

Creating connections between different parties will bring the most value if everyone's potential contributions are recognized and employed. Leadership therefore needs to foster a norm that such forms of knowledge need to be gathered and shared in an active way. Such sharing is achieved more easily if people listen to each other. Only then is room given for communication to take place and, hence, information surfaces more easily. Once the information is there to be picked up, the talking starts. Talking about what we know will help to integrate all knowledge available and motivate performance. It is in this interplay, between listening and talking, that we find inclusive and purpose-driven leadership to work together.

- **Emphasize the importance of other perspectives**

A listening attitude assumes that one takes the perspective of the other party. Although not the same, a strong tendency to take the perspective of others helps to engender an empathetic response to what these others say. Taking the perspective of someone else can help you to cognitively understand what is said and why it matters to this other party. Empathy is the emotional ability to feel what drives the other party to say the things he or she is saying. And, isn't the combination of *I hear you* and *I feel you* the best strategy to connect?

- **Encourage exchange of feedback**

Bringing different parties together goes beyond one-time encounters. When parties are connected, the aim is to build a long-term relationship that facilitates continuous growth, and hence creates greater value over time. For this reason, a common understanding of each other is needed, but over time, this understanding will also need to be updated. Therefore, in the act of connecting, a norm also needs to be installed that the different parties provide feedback to each other. Feedback is a learning tool that parties can use to gain a deeper understanding of the other and thus grow a stronger connection. It helps to correct where needed and improve on what is working.

Trustworthy leadership

It is no secret that people join groups and feel connected with others more easily when trust exists. Trust serves as a social lubricant, or glue, and therefore facilitates co-operation and co-ordination between different parties. Because this wisdom is considered so obvious, a consequence is that many of us do not think consciously about the necessity to continuously create, build and maintain trust anymore. It is only when trust ceases to exist that we suddenly see that all the positive benefits of an inclusive work context do not materialize. As the famous investor, Warren Buffett, once noted, "Trust is like the air we breathe – when it's present, nobody really notices. When it's absent, everyone notices."

It is only when trust is absent that we act, which, of course, is not the most effective way to deal with distrust. Rather, it is better for leaders to be aware that trust needs to be created in almost every action they undertake, as this is the secret to building committed and inclusive teams over time. In other words, leaders need to realize that trust cannot be delegated, leaders need to take responsibility for building it.

Obviously, this reality requires leaders to have the skills to build trust. And, as with many things in life, being able to do so starts with understanding what trust is. In the social sciences, trust is usually defined in a way that addresses the subjective nature of the trust process by emphasizing the beliefs and expectations people have about each other. Therefore, it is often said that trust is in the eye of the beholder.[189]

These beliefs, in turn, influence the display of trusting behavior. Let us take a look at the most commonly used definition of trust that social science scholars use. For them, trust is "a psychological state comprising the intention to accept vulnerability based upon positive expectations of the intentions or behavior of another."[190] So, if people believe that the other party is competent, honest and not motivated to exploit you, then people are willing to take the risk of being vulnerable with the other party. And, if people are willing to be vulnerable in the presence of others, then they will engage in more positive behaviors. Indeed, a vast number of studies over the years have shown that once employees trust each other, they are more likely to co-operate, share information, and feel happier and more satisfied in their job and in their relationships with others.[191,192]

Trust building starts with the leader

Assuming that inclusive work cultures rely on the existence of trusting relationships, leaders are expected to signal – by means of their actions – that they can be trusted. It is up to the leader to take the initiative and start building an impression of trust across the company (remember trust cannot be delegated!). Although this may seem obvious to many, the question of who starts the trust building process is, in reality, not an easy one. Too often, those who are willing to volunteer to take the risk of being exploited are few and far between. The result is that we all end up waiting for somebody else to take the first step. What happens then?

If no one takes the first step, we transfer our hope to a third-party system. Such a system is usually a monitoring or other kind of control system. When such control systems are present, we feel confident that others will not exploit us, because they are being monitored. But, is this really the trust we are talking about, that inclusive leaders need? *Not really.*

Granted, when a control system is present, we trust the reliability and accuracy of the system itself. However, that does not mean that we will now also trust the actions of others. After all, a control system is used to monitor – and maybe even punish – non-co-operative actions of others. Out of fear of punishment, people will collaborate. However, they will not do so because they really want to work together, rather because they have been forced to. So, what do we really know about the intentions of these others when a control system is present? Nothing, really, and this is a problem when it comes down to building trust.

Inclusive leadership deals with the ability to bring people together and create value out of the diverse sampling of individuals who are put together in a group. This requires people to be genuinely interested in each other and therefore trust the other person. Obviously, this requires a kind of trust that is different than the so-called trust installed by a control system. We need trust where people are willing to be vulnerable towards each other and build relationships on shared values, respect and willingness to collaborate. To move groups of individuals to this space, leadership is required to model this kind of behavior. Indeed, we know that effective leaders lead by example. If you, as a leader, display what needs to be done, others will follow and adopt the same kind of mindset.

So how do leaders' model trustworthy behavior? They do so by showing their vulnerability. How do you show vulnerability? By giving trust to others in a risky situation. In fact, we know from research that if a leader is willing to invest their trust in others, most people will reciprocate.[193] This is the reason why they say, trust breeds trust. As a leader, you must set the standard for how people in the organization should act. The norm is to give trust to each other, and thus build a co-operative work setting. Of course, once trust is initiated it needs to be developed and shaped further.

The art of fostering trust

How do you keep building trust? You need to be perceived as trustworthy.[194] Don't forget, trust is in the eye of the beholder, so people will perceive you as a genuine trust builder if they see you as a trustworthy person. Your perceived trustworthiness is used to signal your reputation within the organization. So, it is basically in everyone's interest to promote and maintain one's (perceived) trustworthiness. How to do so? What is the magic formula?

Research has shown that there are three dimensions that are particularly relevant in this respect. The first dimension concerns information about your *competence*. People want to know whether you have the competencies to do your job well. As a leader, you are expected to achieve results and know what others are doing. Of course, competence is very much related to your specific expertise, and therefore is of *relative* significance to people. That is, a doctor is assumed to be an expert on health, but we do not expect this same doctor to be an expert in fixing your car. So, competence is very domain specific. Also, seeing someone as competent is a flexible notion, meaning that humans assume that competencies can be learnt. So, if someone does not have the necessary competencies, we believe this can be solved by training and education. Information about your competencies is usually found out very quickly.

A second dimension of trustworthiness may take longer to discover, since it concerns the dimension of *integrity*. Integrity refers to our values and sense of justice. Leaders with integrity are purpose driven and aware of the values they want to pursue. A peculiar thing about integrity is that it is not seen as a flexible notion; if we see people violate standards of justice and display dishonest behaviors, we quickly feel that they must be a bad person.

Interestingly, once established, it is very difficult to change this negative perception. We mainly adhere to the expression, "once a bad person, always a bad person." The reason for this inflexibility is that we assume that our own personal principles are reflected in our actions towards others. If you exhibit bad behavior, then people will assume that this is the kind of person you are. This is why it is often said that leaders need to *walk the talk*. Inconsistent behavior suggests doubtful integrity.

The third and final dimension shaping people's perceptions of trustworthiness is *benevolence*. Benevolent leaders are seen as those who take care of the interests of others. It is the dimension that underlies the development of positive and healthy relationships. So, benevolent leaders act as a social glue, bringing people closer and more firmly together because they focus on the interests of everyone.

How to develop your trustworthiness

Trustworthy leaders act in ways that lead others to conclude that you are:

- **A competent individual**

Leaders need to be trusted to deliver. The most direct way to assess this is to show that you are successful in executing decisions and achieving results. Results are often dictated by the demands of the situation; in an automated work environment, leaders need to be able to understand what the technological challenges are that lie ahead and demonstrate how they will tackle those challenges. It is important that leaders do not overpromise; promises sound good, but they also raise expectations. If the delivery fails, so too will trust.

Leaders therefore need to show that they are tech savvy and that this knowledge will help them to make the right strategic decision. Again, as I noted earlier, it does not require leaders to be coders, but rather to be aware of the challenges raised by the technological revolution we are witnessing today. In a way, leaders in the 21st century show competence by bringing the right teams of experts together to optimise the use of data to bring the value that is expected.

For example, leaders connecting teams of data scientists with HR and finance teams in transparent and effective ways can help to increase the success rate of digital transformation strategies. The team of data scientists will help their colleagues to see what possibilities are available to digitalize information. Equally, the other teams can help data scientists understand their needs and thus provide input in designing a more user-friendly digital environment. Finally, because successes are rarely achieved immediately, it is important that leaders provide regular updates to the different parties involved on how the challenges are being approached. Even though people have the tendency to look at the actual outcome to infer whether one is competent or not, information about the progress also helps in making favorable impressions regarding your competence.

- **A high integrity individual**

It is crucial that people perceive their leaders as honest and driven by the right values. In an automated work environment, this is especially important when collecting data, since many sensitivities exist about its use. Why is data being collected, how will it be used and will privacy be protected?

The type of behavior that can promote integrity includes open and honest communication to ensure that others are informed about the use of technology and its purpose. It also includes *walking the talk*, as people expect your actions to be in line with what you have promised. Not being able to live up to the expectations that you put out there will severely damage your reputation, as people will doubt your intentions and promises. Finally, being a person of high integrity also means you must have a respectful attitude towards others. People trust leaders who treat others as human beings with their own unique abilities – regardless of the outcomes that have been achieved. In being able to distinguish the process (how you treat people) from the results (how you reward people), leaders can show themselves as individuals that value and respect the worth of others.

- **A benevolent individual**

At the end of the day, people want to feel that their interests are protected and taken care of. Leaders are also judged on whether they care about and support their employees when they face challenges at work. Especially in the rapidly developing work environments of today's automation era, employees want to feel secure. It is not the case that with more technology, we will have to show less human care towards others. No, it is exactly the opposite! Obviously, such challenges will take more of your time and demand more of your effort, but enlightened leaders need to be prepared for this.

Also, the process of implementing new technology is far from perfect, as witnessed by many digital transformation failures. In those moments, leaders can make a difference in the lives of employees by offering a sympathetic acknowledgement that the digital transformation process can sometimes be difficult and disruptive.

- **An individual who communicates in transparent ways**

When change sets in, the complexity and pace of work also rises. For leaders, it will be important to have the change process accompanied by transparent and clear communication. The importance of transparent communication will only increase in today's data-driven organizations. A greater sense of data transparency is required to ensure that everyone knows what data is available and what will be done with it.

Today's technology revolution requires a more open and de-centralized approach to work. As such, employees today do not accept that an ever-increasing amount of data will be centralized and placed under the control of only a few managers. Data transparency practices in the 21st century require an open access policy to build trust. If data transparency is low, the integrity of the organization is quickly doubted, and suspicion and distrust will set in almost immediately.

Diversity-minded leadership

When bringing people together in a group, the similarities and differences between individuals immediately become obvious. What do you do with the differences that exist? Do we have to consider them disruptive, or do these differences have some value to the collective?

The latter is correct. It is the value of diversity. Societies and its organizations emphasize diversity as an important value that we should respect. The focus on diversity is one of the reasons why inclusive leadership has become widely endorsed. Inclusive leaders recognize the value of diversity and use such differing points of view to both achieve their vision and create more value.

The diversity curator

The ability to appreciate different perspectives may actually be *the* skill needed in the future. Management thinker Lynda Gratton, a professor of practice at the London Business School, recently pointed out that one of the jobs of the future will be the diversity curator. The role will be to actively seek new perspectives, learn from failures as he/she experiments, and promote the effectiveness and adaptability of the organization. This makes a lot of sense, especially so if we look at the need for leadership to empower both humans and algorithms in their tasks while simultaneously converging their efforts to create value for their organization.

Inclusive leadership also requires leaders to embrace diversity. Inclusive leaders are able to think of diversity as a strength, rather than a weakness, and should therefore experiment with and learn from diversity. This should result in a strong set of *diversity beliefs*. These beliefs refer to a sense of awareness that diversity can bring benefits as well as possible conflicts to group functioning.[195] Such a sense of awareness translates into the belief that diversity serves the promotion of inclusiveness.

Experiment and fail

But, of course, leadership does not simply end with this belief. Something has to be done with it! In this respect, it is also important to be aware that diversity can potentially reveal both positive and negative consequences for the collective. As an inclusive leader, you have to take an active approach to experiment with diversity and have the ability to deal with failure. When failure does occur, it is important that you *do not* give up on diversity. After all, the most important thing will be to learn from it. And, let's face it, it is almost a given that within a developing automated work context, it will be inevitable that digital implementation will fail from time to time.

Under those circumstances, we need leaders that have the patience and willingness to experiment, but who will also show compassion to their workforce. In fact, inclusive and compassionate leadership align well if the aim is to promote a diverse workforce. Compassionate leaders are known to make others in the workplace feel safe, which is a prerequisite to engaging in experiments. Neuroimaging research has in fact shown that compassionate leaders build the trust needed to translate diversity into effective work relationships and make employees display high loyalty to those leaders showing compassion.[196,197]

How to develop your diversity mindset

With an increasingly automated workplace, new challenges will emerge, new types of employees will arrive, and new ways of working need to be explored. Under these circumstances, leaders need to be able to bring all aspects of the new work culture together, which entails cultivating a mindset that puts diversity to good use. To achieve this kind of thinking, leaders need to:

- **Understand the value of diversity**

  When pursuing a vision, leaders are faced with many decisions. These decisions are becoming increasingly complicated within the work context of the new diversity. This new environment – where humans and machines are colleagues – raises the need for leaders to ensure that when making an important decision, they look at it from different angles. Diversity helps to make salient different perspectives for the same problem. Therefore, recognizing that diversity can be a strength in your decision-making process in reality means that you truly understand the value of having a diverse work force.

  To acquire such an understanding, I suggest that leaders in the 21st century should take an active approach to seeking out new perspectives within the work context. Leaders need to train themselves to integrate the known facts and needs of different parties, with the values that the organization wants to create. This kind of training requires a continuous effort to gather information from different parties with the aim of fostering a habit of engaging in *meta-thinking*. It is the development of meta-thinking that makes leaders effective, both because it helps to understand the value of the perspectives that different parties adopt, and to integrate the different perspectives into a comprehensive action plan that makes sense in light of the more general vision.

- **Promote agile thinking**

  Recognizing the value of diverse perspectives is one thing, but one also needs to make effective use of this knowledge. We live in what is often called a VUCA world: volatile, uncertain, complex and ambiguous.

Because of the introduction of algorithms in the business world, business has become much more difficult to execute. As a result, leaders need to create a culture where the introduction of new technology is met with a willingness to learn. This kind of learning culture ensures that technical knowledge is constantly distributed in order to optimise cross-functional team work.[198] The skill of being comfortable with change motivates leaders to consider problems and change from different angles.

- **Be aware of biased perceptions**

As humans, we are not rational beings. Our irrational nature makes us vulnerable to biases in our judgments and decisions. This is especially the case when it comes down to dealing with situations of diversity. Research has shown that we can easily be biased in preferring one perspective over another. We often do so because deep inside (on a subconscious level) we favor one group over another and this implicit belief ultimately influences our decisions and actions.

It is easy to see that humans may run the risk of always favoring the human perspective above the algorithmic one. And this may sometimes be a valid assumption, but we need to make sure that because of our biases we do not lose the added value provided by algorithms. Leaders of tomorrow thus need to be cognizant of these biases and train themselves to be aware of how they react towards the presence of different parties. A first task is therefore to try eliminating the biased preferences that can be consciously identified. The second task is to grow your awareness of biased perceptions and try to recognize where you display such unconscious biases. This second step requires you to put certain decision policies, processes and structures in place to shield you against these unconscious tendencies, preferably starting with having people around you who constantly remind you of other perspectives.

Humble leadership

Leadership that includes and connects all parties is celebrated because of its open attitude to diversity. In addition, it is credited with being able to see strength in difference, while not being afraid to experiment with these diverse approaches. For such inclusive leadership to emerge, leaders are expected to create psychologically safe work climates where prejudice and bias are absent. If trust is present, then differences are more easily accepted, discussed and embraced. As a result, different ways of working will be explored and the likelihood for success will increase. We could even conclude that if prejudice exists, then less opportunities will be created.

Please challenge me!

Of course, creating value for all is not an easy thing to achieve. It requires you, as a leader, to be critical of the assumptions you hold. In a way, you should be your own devil's advocate. In my classes with executives, I often emphasize that when they launch initiatives and experience no push-back from others, they owe it to themselves to criticize their own initiatives. Many of them are surprised when I say this and wonder why they should criticize their own ideas. If everyone agrees with it, isn't that the best outcome?

Of course, we all like our ideas to go unchallenged. However, if no one challenges you, it usually means something else. It means there is no trust, or that people do not feel safe to speak up. Or, even worse, that people feel it is a waste of time to challenge you, because you will not listen. If you fail to see this, then it means you are not open minded enough, nor attentive enough, to the social dynamic in your team. Worst of all, it may reflect a lack of humility.

Promoting bottom-up thinking

Social scientists define humility as "letting one's accomplishments speak for themselves; not seeking the spotlight; [and] not regarding oneself as more special than one is."[199] It is a moral value that motivates people to be open to the opinion of others while at the same time being critical about one's own assumptions. With such an attitude, you are less self-focused, which helps you to make better choices when a wider range of opportunities presents itself.

In fact, humility is a key component of effective leadership in increasingly dynamic and turbulent environments.[200] Under such circumstances, organizations need leaders who act quickly in exploring different perspectives and draw from the wide range of wisdom available. And this is exactly what humble leaders do.

For example, when it comes down to seeking the opinions of others, research has demonstrated that leaders with a humble attitude stimulate bottom-up dynamics in teams and throughout their organization.[201] In other words, humble leaders do not shy away from admitting what they do not know. As a result, they are big fans of the bottom-up cycle, where ideas at the lower levels move upwards and influence the organization.

How to develop your humility?

Humble leaders are aware of what they know and what they do not know. This helps them to create a collaborative culture. Humble leaders are able to:

• **Adopt a broad perspective**
People usually like to stick to what they already know and keep acting in routine ways. Our biological make-up does not encourage us to explore other ways of thinking and acting. Instead, most of us develop a mindset that others are likely to think and act like us. Indeed, humans are very good at denying the idea that much diversity in thinking and acting exists out there. Humble leaders acknowledge that people do not always think and act like themselves. They are able to shift their attention away from their own point of view and focus on the ideas, perceptions and views of those around them.

• **Listen to others**
Being aware of your strengths and weaknesses instils the motivation to see and hear how others think and act. Of course, admitting your weaknesses in the first place requires you to be willing and able to make yourself vulnerable. It requires that you tone down the perfect image that we all like to shape for ourselves. Humble leaders are realistic enough to recognise the limitations of their own abilities and, as such, are more willing to turn to others to ask for their input and help. The trick here is to realize that admitting weakness and asking others for help does not communicate a sign of failure, but rather a sign of great character.

• **Admit their mistakes**
All leaders are human, which means they all make mistakes from time to time. When you are willing to share your own missteps, it allows others to connect with you in a deeper and more authentic way. If your

habit, however, is to do everything within your power to portray yourself as perfect, then people will actually look at you as inhuman. As a result, you will create distance, not loyalty or commitment. Being humble as a leader is thus a quality that lets others see your humanity which in turn promotes connection.

Summary: The benefits of inclusive leadership

With a new player (i.e. algorithms) entering the organizational setting, an open-minded and collaborative mindset is needed more than ever to ensure that the implementation of technology creates the value that we expect. The emphasis on inclusive thinking and acting is therefore a requirement for any organization where automation is adopted, because it allows for:

Different departments to co-operate

A common problem for most companies is the existence of silos. Many people perceive their job in terms of the targets they need to obtain, and as such do not go beyond their own job requirements. It means that departments only stick to what they *need* to do. They tick all their own boxes, but rarely the boxes of other departments. The end result is that it is difficult for companies to work in a collaborative way, where all knowledge present in the organization is brought together to help make the best decisions. With algorithms entering the workforce, the risk exists that this silo phenomenon will only become more pervasive.

When it comes to using algorithms, the risks that silos bring are two-fold. First, departments will use algorithms in different ways, meaning no comprehensive point of view will be developed on how the organization as a whole should employ them to serve the purpose of the company. Second, some departments will employ algorithms more than others, thereby creating differences in work attitudes towards automation, which will make the process of digital transformation more difficult.

Integrating teams of data scientists in the daily operations of the company

With the work environment gradually being automated, organizations will increasingly hire more people with an engineering and data-science background. These new hires will have an expert understanding of the new technology and the ability to work with big data. A problem, however, is that those experts usually do not share the same mindset as the people who are not trained in the fields of engineering and data science. Organizations often fail to recognize this difference in mindset and put little effort into ensuring that data scientists are integrated into the organization.

Becoming an automated organization means that all operations will be affected. Teams of data scientists thus need to understand the goals of the finance department, human resource department, sales department and so forth. Likewise, organizations need to prepare all the other departments to be open and collaborative with the team of data scientists. It is only with an open-minded attitude that successful integration and implementation of algorithms within the context of each department can be achieved.[202]

Promoting transparency in communication and exchange of data

Today there is no longer any doubt that to succeed in the future, organizations will need to have the ability to deal with data and use algorithms. A first step is to ensure that data is captured and stored in user-friendly and accessible ways. A second step involves making this data available to everyone, which implies the democratization of data.

This first step is relatively easy to do, but the second often fails because of a lack of inclusive leadership. Indeed, once the technology is fully implemented, a major problem is usually a lack of collaboration between people, which is necessary for the automation efforts to succeed. A more inclusive work environment makes information more easily accessible and shared. So, a transparency policy with regard to data management requires that individuals, teams and departments communicate with each other and that the organizational leadership facilitates a collaborative mindset.

Empower algorithms in non-biased ways

With an inclusive mindset in place, algorithms will be more easily seen as co-workers. They will be recognized as being part of the same team as you are! To achieve this level of inclusion it is necessary to create a sense of connection with the algorithm rather than a sense of distance. An inclusive work culture helps with this ambition. Inclusive leaders foster this work culture by helping employees to understand the value of the algorithm. They can do this by creating continuous education opportunities to understand advancements in technology.

Be humble, and work on being tech savvy

The presence of algorithms may create discrepancies in technological knowledge between different departments. Leaders therefore need to create a safe and trustworthy climate where people can address their lack of understanding when it comes to new technology. Such a climate can help to build a culture where employees help each other in this area of expertise. In addition, such an enlightened work climate will also help the organization to identify which departments need more training to help them understand the value of algorithms to achieve the overall goals of the company.

CHAPTER 10
What Will Be and What Should Be

A I IS TOUTED as the next hero in our ever-changing society. Heroes are used in movies to reveal the qualities that we are missing, and, in this, AI is no exception. Indeed, driven by a limitless ambition to optimize our own abilities, our society has moved quickly towards adopting algorithms. In fact, we have invented so many of them that today they seem to be used for every application imaginable.

The primary strength of algorithms is their ability to process a vast amount of data at high speed and reveal trends and insights that humans without technological support would not necessarily see. For obvious reasons, this is an excellent skill when it comes down to improving (or some may say perfecting) how our society works. In 2009, Lloyd Blankfein, chairman and chief executive of Goldman Sachs, said that bankers do the work of God. Well, this time around, it seems like we have catapulted algorithms to a level where they are not only taking over the role of bankers, but maybe even God!

This God-like status of AI has not escaped the attention of organizations either. They are rational, focused, systematic in their processing and more accurate than any human can ever be. In the eyes of corporate executives, algorithms make the perfect advisor to the decision-making process within organizations. One could even say that algorithms are being recognized as tools that maintain a *cool head*, helping organizations to make decisions void of sentiment: the perfect decision-making machine! While all of this may be true, I think we all realize that, at the end of the day, organizations are likely to need more than a *cool* approach to succeed. Instead, more often than not, they are also in need of a *warm* approach.

A so-called *warm* approach comes along with the right sentiments to assess the importance of different stakeholder's interests in the decisions that need to be made. Today, more than ever, organizations need to be very much aware of the kind of social value they want to create by means of their decisions.

In fact, in the summer of 2019, the Business Roundtable, led by JPMorgan Chase CEO Jamie Dimon and including leaders from some of America's biggest companies, announced that decisions made by organizations should not only reflect the interests of shareholders, but of all stakeholders. With this statement, companies have now officially left behind the ideas developed by the famous economist Milton Friedman, who argued in his article, 'The social responsibility of business is to increase its profits,' that the sole purpose of an organization is to maximize profit for the shareholder.[203] In a way, Friedman is saying that promoting shareholder value is the ethical thing to do!

Today, we know better. Confronted with the possibility of becoming a more tech-driven and thus *cool* society, we increasingly feel that we need more, rather than less, humanity. In addition to rational calculations and optimal functions derived from further data analysis, we are feeling the need to emphasize the importance of sound and ethical judgments that satisfy the concerns and needs of all those being implicated by the decision taken. Such a realistic perspective stresses the necessity for organizations and their respective leaders to be constantly aware during their digital transformation journeys of both the opportunities and limitations that algorithms bring to the table.

Too good to be true?

The first issue that we need to resolve is that the idea of digital transformation does not signal the end of human activity in the workplace. Yet feelings of fear have nevertheless gone up since algorithms started penetrating organizational reality. By now, it should be clear that the omnipresence of algorithms in combination with deep learning processes is regarded by today's company leaders as the most effective business model. This model allows for organizations to pursue amazing possibilities that both drive execution costs down and promote effectiveness and work performance. In fact, evidence abounds that corporate executives today are fully embracing the idea that it is an automated workforce that should be relied upon to excel in the future. And why wouldn't they? Just think about it: paying less and getting more! It does sound like a great deal, does it not? But, let us ask ourselves whether it could be a case of sounding too good to be true? Or, stated differently, could it be that in our corporate enthusiasm, we seem to be forgetting something?

That *little* thing we may be forgetting concerns the realization that embracing the idea of optimization, and hence, a likely desire to create a perfect world, we run the risk of losing our human identity in the process. In fact, this is not really a little thing at all. The initial idea behind our efforts to let algorithmic presence grow in our organizations is and should always be to optimize the workings of a *humane* society. The idea is not, and should never be, to upgrade and implement AI at such a level that we ultimately forget to serve the human aspect of our quickly developing society.

The end user is human – not technology. We do not innovate AI-applications to create a society where the end user becomes the algorithm itself. If we were to do so, then we would have to conclude that the goal driving today's AI-revolution is to develop the most perfect technology possible – without regard for the kind of society we will be creating. Even more so, if this is really the case, then we are developing technology solely for the sake of making technology perfect, and nothing else. And, then, dear reader, the end user of this AI-driven revolution is indeed the algorithm itself.

The end user is technology, or am I wrong?

Some of you may say that it will never go this far. But may I offer a parallel example to clarify that the question I just introduced may actually be more real than we think. Without a doubt you will remember the controversy in 2018 where it was revealed that the data of as many as 87 million Facebook users were accessed and used for both research and political purposes. The founder and CEO of Facebook, Mark Zuckerberg, received much criticism and people wondered whether he realized the importance of privacy to human users.

Indeed, the end users here are humans, like you and me, so why was he being so inconsiderate in how their data was used? Was he not aware that he – as creator – was responsible not only for ensuring technological progress, but also for the welfare of his customers? To answer this question, let us rewind to June 2017, where Mark Zuckerberg, in an interview with Freakonomics Radio said: "Of course, privacy is extremely important, and people engage and share their content and feel free to connect because they know that their privacy is going to be protected [on Facebook]."

Great! The creator of Facebook knew that privacy matters to the human end user and should be treated with care. But, only one year later, it became clear that he was not really treating privacy and the value it carries for humans with much care. What became clear instead is that people like Mark Zuckerberg were primarily driven by the ambition to innovate and show off rapid technological development (remember how *cool* it makes your company), rather than thinking about the consequences it may have for the kind of society that will be created. Zuckerberg suffers from what I call an *innovation only* bias.[204] He wants to innovate to serve the goal of innovation itself. Innovate to innovate! Such a bias can be called a blind spot, because it shows that if we are obsessed with creating something unique that seems to have almost unlimited possibilities, we only come to see the value of the innovation itself. And often the consequences revealed are to the detriment of its end user and society at large.

This is exactly what happened in the case of Facebook. It was only when Mark Zuckerberg was forced by his court hearings to think about his own role in the technological innovation, that he realized he was also responsible for the consequences that a platform such as Facebook reveals to the welfare and interest of its human users. As he said: "I started [Facebook], I run it, I'm responsible for what happens here. I'm not looking to throw anyone else under the bus for mistakes that we've made here."

Eventually, he got it. In his striving for the next technological improvement, he did not consider the perspective of the human and the values (privacy) involved. Only when tragedy hit his company, was he forced to take the perspective of the human end user as well.

I believe that at this moment the parallel between the Facebook case and our current obsession with developing an ever more perfect algorithm, powered on by deep learning processes we do not understand anymore, has become painstakingly clear. We are innovating for the sake of innovation, which may actually serve technology more rather than humanity. The risk may well be (as it was clearly so in the Facebook case) that we only realize we have handed over control to a perfect technology system, and thus lost our humanity, when it is too late. To prevent this, it is necessary that we bring this kind of debate into the picture as soon as possible. We must also ensure that any organization, government, and society implementing new technology in an effort to optimize their functioning, should always be aware (and to some extent be reminded) to use human welfare as the ultimate goal in our efforts to automate.

What about the human?

Let me put it this way: although these concerns were not a consideration when AI started its upsurge, today serious doubts are arising when it concerns this issue. In fact, when we listen carefully, most opposition against the increasing trend to automatize almost always involves typical human concerns and fears. Very few concerns are being raised about potential limitations of the technology itself. The sky is the limit when it comes down to forecasting how technology may develop. However, with this optimistic view on the potential and abilities of technology itself, fears and doubts arise regarding the future of our human identity.

The more mature and autonomously acting algorithms grow, the more humanity seems to become a challenging issue. For example, we notice that although automation is setting in, promising opportunities we can hardly imagine today, many employees continue to be afraid. They are afraid of working with the new technology, afraid to recognize the algorithmic functioning of their new co-workers, and afraid that all of this may lead to their redundancy. In essence, people are starting to say: "What about me, the human?"

This existential fear has come to the surface as a sense of algorithm aversion. As mentioned, algorithms are perceived as black boxes, meaning that humans have a hard time trusting them. After all, if your new co-worker is increasingly having a say, but you do not know how this co-worker thinks, then fear will automatically set in. And these negative feelings will not be easy to dismiss, especially as design engineers begin to have an increasingly hard time explaining how algorithms work themselves.

This reality opens the door to the possibility that AI-driven technology may as well grow from a rather narrow type of intelligence – only focusing on the task at hand – to a type of intelligence that will not only match the unique strength of human intelligence, but surpass it.

If the designer, who is human, is limited in their understanding of how technology functions, then it is inevitable that human dependence on new technology will not only increase, but become a fact of life. Such a reality will also ensure that technology's dependence on human input will decrease at an alarming rate. This will transpire in a change of the position and influence of humans within organizations, societies and the world at large.

Although a reality where a super type of AI liberates itself entirely from human influence still sounds very futuristic to many, and is unlikely to happen in the next few decades, it should make us aware that we need to start thinking about our own position towards algorithms in the next stage of organizational development.

We will survive... again!

It is these kind of innate reflections – activated whenever humanity comes under threat – that make people increasingly worry about algorithms being part of the workforce. As these human fears seem to be specific to our biological make-up, we could well say that opposition to the massive use of algorithms in organizations is nothing really new. Indeed, as critics will argue, every time a revolution is started to challenge our way of working, our own biological reality leads humans to experience existential fears.

But whenever these existential fears come to the surface, humans nevertheless seem to be able to adapt and move on. As such, one may suggest that the truly unique ability of humans is to survive. And we do so, again and again, because of our ability to adapt. It is an ability so dear to our biological make-up that Charles Darwin wrote an entire book on it.[205] One of the key arguments that Darwin introduces in his book, *On the Origin of Species*, is that individuals who can adapt most to the environment at hand will be most likely to survive and thus reproduce.

According to Darwin, humans (not all of them, though) have the capacity to adjust to any change in the environment, and it is this innate desire and motivation that allows the human species to survive over time. Building on this, we should be relatively confident that the human species will find a way to adapt to an increasingly automated environment. However, what kind of shape this adaptation will have to take is less clear. Will humans occupy a submissive role towards algorithms, or a role where man becomes part of machine? At this moment, no one knows. But the main message seems to be of cautious optimism: humans are likely to survive anything.

But, before we ride out to victory with an unshaken belief that man will survive whatever the threat, let me issue a warning. I believe that what we are talking about today is something other than the average threat humanity has encountered before. Today, a discussion is taking shape where we are talking about a revolution that in reality may not have much of a future for humans. In its most extreme form, the end of the road may well be near for humans.

After all, does the popular press and tech gurus worldwide not speak of a technology that will grow to becoming a better and stronger version of the human species? If these forecasts materialize, then it will be the first time in history that we will not be equipped to remain the dominant species on this planet. We will become followers of a system superior to ourselves and, maybe, in the second instance, even become eliminated. The fact that such possibilities are seriously being envisioned, means that we owe it to ourselves to be responsible enough to discuss and reflect upon how we want to use this new technology within our societies.

Co-operation above all

One aspect of this task involves looking at how both humans and algorithms simultaneously (and thus in co-operation) play a role in the organization of the future. Co-operation is the one thing that has allowed the human species to survive while it found new ways of dealing with change. In other words, the act of co-operation implies a sense of awareness that for future welfare to emerge, all parties are needed with all their unique abilities and strengths. This will create greater opportunities to come up with new and innovative ways to face the future, but in a way that is directed and guided by human concerns.

It is this kind of innovation that will bring us the best chance for humanity to adapt and thus survive. As such, we are today faced with the important task of implementing new ways to co-operate that best utilize both humans and technology. This *new diversity* will therefore aim to pave the path to a better, more efficient society, one that preserves and stimulates human identity.

In this context, such optimization does not then aim to develop technology beyond human boundaries. Instead, it involves applying new technology in such a way that it promotes and enhances human survival in the most efficient way possible. And, because of that, development of new technology is guided, even tempered, by its main goal: to help advance humanity. In light of this, we need to determine limits for the tech revolution before it is too late and the distance between algorithms and humans becomes a gap impossible to bridge.

Of course, to achieve such a collaborative situation, all parties involved need to have the right attitude. A sense of realism is needed to pinpoint the problems that exist today and address them with human concern as the primary focus. So, where are we today with this particular ambition?

The current state of affairs seems to be that a disconnect exists between the perceptions of those wanting to use the new technology (corporate leaders and shareholders), to promote their company's interests, and the employees working in that same company. This disconnect not only creates tension, which makes algorithm implementation even more difficult, but brings to the fore the view that the automation process itself is perceived as a real (existential) threat to the human face of organizations. These are serious matters which need to be dealt with in cautionary ways. Research conducted by PwC revealed that 90% of C-suite executives indicated that their companies are paying attention to people's needs when introducing new technology.[206]

At this moment, we could conclude that even though automation of the workforce is the business model to work with, corporate leaders do seem to take the human cause seriously. But, before we breathe a sigh of relief, PwC's findings also revealed another side to the story. The same survey found that only 53% of employees agreed with the assessment of the C-suite executives. As such, these findings underscore a discrepancy between the perception of our corporate leaders and their employees when it comes down to how new technology should be treated.

How to move on

What to think of this discrepancy? In my view, rather than launching an investigation into who's right and who's wrong, a constructive debate is needed where both perceived realities are embraced and brought together. On the one hand, the law of innovation that new ideas and trends are inevitable dictates that automation has set in and is here to stay. The best thing then would appear to be to embrace the potential of new technology and explore further how it can function in optimal ways within the organizational context.

On the other hand, anyone who has children also knows that simply forcing others to accept things and do as they are told does not help things either. Employees therefore need to be given the opportunity to learn and test the innovative potential of new technology in light of the progress that humanity seeks. Such a testing phase should allow for corrections to take place. Important to the cause of striving for an improved sense of human identity, it should also provide assurance to us that human leadership (and not followership) will remain in place.

As mentioned, organizations need to take the first step towards building a work culture that allows for co-operation between humans and algorithms to take place. Co-operation is important to organizational functioning as it brings together the expertise and contributions of different parties. So, in today's digital society, organizations should see no problem in fostering co-operation between algorithms and human employees. The problem we are facing, however, is that on average people prefer to work more with other humans rather than algorithms. Organizations and their leadership are therefore forced to create the right culture by fostering a digital mindset. This will help to motivate employees to think about the opportunities created by employing algorithms, such as fostering more innovative ideas to help companies grow.

With such a culture in place, we should be able to initiate a virtuous innovation cycle that is defined by the process of co-creation between algorithms and humans. A report by Accenture (2018) suggests that the new technology (AI) is best used in collaboration with humans, since the merging of the unique abilities of both parties will generate better outcomes.[207] Accenture illustrated this idea nicely by referring to the employment of AI techniques by doctors at Harvard to detect breast cancer cells. AI itself scored 92% accuracy, but human pathologists nevertheless did better by achieving 96% accuracy. It was only when both partners found a way to collaborate that the detection rate rose to 99.5%.

Building the right culture

If we want to survive this new revolution, then organizations should not hesitate to build a culture that ensures that the implementation of algorithms will lead to successful co-creation with humans. This task does not seem too difficult, does it?

Well, unfortunately, it does. First of all, a recent survey from Microsoft in Asia revealed that organizations today are failing to install a mindset that leads employees to accept and engage AI.[208] In fact, the survey stated explicitly that the Asia Pacific is not ready yet for AI. And, why is this?

Isn't it the case that we are witnessing a technology race between the US and China which is predicted to expose the differences between Eastern and Western technology approaches? As such, the world should be ready for the arrival of new technology. So, what is missing? It turns out that building the right culture seems to be a key barrier. Among the Asia Pacific business leaders interviewed for the survey, more than half indicated that companies today are failing to build a culture and corresponding mindset that recognizes AI as a way to promote innovation. If this is the case, then, obviously, the much-needed co-creation between humans and algorithms will not be facilitated, but rather made more difficult.

Second, this failure to culture build is actually not such a big surprise. Organizational scholars have been discussing the challenge of building the right work culture for decades. The fact that this debate has been going on for so long is an indication of just how hard it is to reach a consensus on what it takes to change culture. In fact, an abundance of models exists outlining what to do when it comes down to cultural transformations. Nevertheless, organizations keep knocking on the doors of both scholars and consultants to help drive their cultural change projects. If there is one thing, however, that seems common to all the cultural change models out there, then it is that to make change happen one party cannot be missed. And, that one party is leaders who display the right kind of leadership to guide change in ways that are meaningful to others.

Leadership is a process of influence that can drive change in how people think and act. For this reason, effective leadership is needed to influence the installation of a mindset that helps humans to recognize the value of the new technology along with its goals. If organizations can think along these lines, a more fertile ground will exist for co-creation between humans and algorithms to take place in more optimal ways. And, with this leadership suggestion, we have arrived at a very interesting point in our discussion on leadership by algorithm.

As you might remember, earlier in this book, I mentioned that human superiority in leading organizations is not immune to the threat of algorithms. The whole construct is advanced by a business model that advocates the use of new technology to help organizations find a better fit with a business environment that is dynamic, complex and volatile.

This idea is recognized by the corporate world and its leaders, to the extent that my executive students are increasingly worried about how automated their leadership position will become in the future. In their minds, they are fearful of a future in which algorithms will take over their leadership. Seeing how dependent we are becoming on algorithms, fuels the idea that human leadership will soon be a thing of the past. In fact, the fear exists that future leadership will be stripped of its human elements. But, if it is true that we need leaders to create a culture that can lead human employees to engage with algorithms, surely the leadership needed for this cannot also be algorithmic in nature?

Human employees need to be inspired to see the value of the new technology. This is unlikely to happen if the source of inspiration is provided by the new technology itself. As I have discussed extensively, algorithms can provide more optimal and systematic ways of looking at reality by analysing data at a level of speed and accuracy no human is able to do so. But, these same algorithms are not able to provide the authentic sense of leadership required to make decisions and subsequent meaningful changes to the humans being led. Building a culture that effects employees' ways of thinking and acting requires a process of logic that connects with our human identity and ambitions.

Humans lead, algorithms manage

What this discussion makes clear is that the leadership of the future should be able to create a culture in which it becomes meaningful for humans to collaborate with non-humans. This empowerment of the *new diversity* requires guidance in such a way that both parties know their position within the work setting and accordingly create value that serves a society defined by humanity rather than by technological innovation.

To achieve this outcome, we need human-driven leadership. In fact, I would go even further to say that it requires a human leader to provide us with a vision and corresponding judgment that can help to stay close to an authentic sense of humanity in an increasingly automated reality. Having said this, at the same time, I do believe (and evidence is pointing in the same direction) that the execution of our ideas by means of adopting agreed-upon procedures and strategies, does not necessarily need a human hand.

The effective management of our procedures – once a vision is communicated and accepted – relies less on the ability to create meaning than on the ability to establish order. For this reason, as I argued earlier, the execution of the management function is very likely to become automated up to a level that management by algorithm will become the default.

Management by algorithm is more or less in line with what we expect from our human management. Today, we expect (human) managers to create order and stability by employing procedures we have designed for this purpose. Algorithms can be used in ways that provide a more optimal and accurate way of managing than humans are capable of. In itself, management by algorithm is also less likely to pose a threat to the more existential concerns of humans, when it comes down to deciding on how dependent to be on an algorithm. In other words, management by algorithm represents less of a threat to the existential fear of losing our human identity when it concerns the issue of how to run an organization. Why am I saying this?

A recent report by the Boston Consulting Group revealed that a majority of employees do not aspire to become a manager.[209] The report also revealed that only one in ten Western non-managers said that they aspire to become a manager. Of the existing managers, the report reveals, only 37% of Western managers say they would like to remain a manager in five to ten years. This trend, in fact, may be good news in light of our argument that management by algorithm is more or less waiting to happen.

As illustrated earlier, most management tasks are likely to become fully automated. However, if employees today are not interested in those management positions anymore, then it seems less likely that humans will be plagued by the existential fear of losing their human identity to the increasing trend of automation. In fact, the situation, as described by the Boston Consulting Group, suggests that there is a close fit between the desires of human managers and the opportunities offered by an increase of automation in organizations. Humans want to do less managing and algorithms are increasingly more equipped to do the managing. A win-win situation seems to be emerging here!

This win-win situation, however, may only materialize if, at the same time, we, as a society, are successful in motivating humans to foster and train the unique human abilities that can allow us to think like leaders and not simply managers. In light of our ambition for continuous education, we can accept management by algorithm, but only if we, as humans, grow our leadership abilities to provide direction and give a sense of meaning to the decisions that we take and will have to take – at all levels of life. It is only then that the combination of algorithms (managing) and humans (leading) will create sustainable value. Why am I saying this so forcefully?

Well, it should be clear by now that we are mistaken if we look to algorithms for direction. They are machines and, as such, not guided by outcomes that are value-driven or meaningful in light of our unique human identity. Rather, algorithms operate within a utilitarian framework which optimizes their actions. A great example of how utilitarian companies really employ their algorithms is the discussion surrounding how the YouTube algorithm makes recommendations to viewers. The metric that YouTube uses to decide on their recommendations for you as a customer (i.e. watch time) is not aimed at helping customers to get what they want, but rather to maximize their engagement – and, hence, make them addicted – without any other consideration.[210]

Despite all the promising narratives floating around that AI will soon surpass human competence across the board, and as such that any human task will come into reach of algorithms (including leadership), reality shows a different face. As Melanie Mitchell writes in her book, *Artificial Intelligence: A Guide for Thinking Humans*, algorithms can achieve excellent levels of performance within the context of narrowly defined tasks, but in essence they are useless when it comes down to providing meaning within the broader context.[211] According to Mitchell, this is the case because algorithms do not have common sense. If we adopt this point of view, then it becomes clear that algorithms cannot provide advice or any judgment about what the value of each outcome means to our human society. Indeed, algorithms are simply not able to assess the value created by means of their decisions and actions in light of its contribution to humanity.

Who knows where to go?

Leaders are required to think in terms of how contributions by the collective can create value for humanity. Leadership is out there to drive change and this process does not simply imply a transactional process without any emotional connection. Rather, leadership builds cultures that are able to achieve progressive outcomes, but at the same preserve a sense of moral and social harmony that allows for co-operation to emerge. Without the ability to create this kind of harmony, leadership cannot drive transformation in successful ways. This realization brings us back to the earlier mentioned idea that it is – and can only be – human leaders who are equipped to create the right mindset for co-operation between humans and algorithms to take place today. So, leadership in the organization of tomorrow remains human at its core exactly because unique human traits bring to the table what is needed for the employment of algorithms in ways that preserves humanity.

The importance of training, educating and promoting humans to lead in a tech-driven society cannot be underestimated; both because human are the most effective leaders, and because human virtues should be used as the basis of our society and organizations in the future. With respect to having the most effective leaders in place, it is clear that the main objective will be to establish the right kind of co-operation between humans and algorithms to ensure co-creation of the highest quality. This process requires leadership that is able to judge the value of the outcomes that result from such co-operation. It is those judgment calls that cannot be replicated by machines and so are considered uniquely human. Indeed, the ability to establish co-operation requires that the one leading the process is knowledgeable and aware of the importance of contributing to the collective good. This collective good is meant to bring welfare and benefits to the members of our organizations and society.

So, how do we ensure that leaders are able to foster such ways of working? This requires leaders to be curious and explore how to extend the boundaries of how our organizations work without sacrificing the human DNA of the society in which those organizations work. Similarly, leaders should be able to imagine what future human welfare should look like and hence be able to take the perspective (understand the emotions, desires and needs of the stakeholders) of the organization we need to create to achieve this purpose. This future-oriented thinking, combined with a strong sense of emotional intelligence and imagination, sets the stage to work in creative ways.

Continuous education

Although in theory nothing should be impossible to imagine, it seems safe to argue that algorithms cannot be fitted within the framework of a human-driven type of leadership. On the contrary, I would say that if we do try to imagine algorithms taking over leadership positions, fear and worry about our human condition will quickly surface. Specifically, when thinking about algorithms performing leadership tasks, many of us fear that this new technology is not sensitive and understanding enough to be able to contribute to the collective good and ensure humanity's progress. Rather, algorithms are better off providing the necessary input to bolster technological developments to speed up human progress. The evaluation of whether the progress achieved is for the benefit of humanity is, however, another question, and requires a deeper understanding of what it means to be human.

Indeed, regardless of the fact that algorithms in several areas seem to be on their way towards matching or even surpassing human intelligence (e.g. detecting tumors, automated driving and so forth), it is undeniable, as Melanie Mitchell writes, that in order to create value for humanity, we still require our human ingenuity. It is therefore no surprise that when it comes down to shaping the leadership of the future, we have an obligation and responsibility to safeguard the human DNA of our leaders. The human DNA in this case stands for the ability to show compassion, forgiveness, empathy, ethical awareness, curiosity and imagination, all virtues that are needed to design tech-driven environments that ensure the promotion of our human identity.

Leadership is needed to bring human sense into today's technology race, where we are employing algorithms at an increasing rate. It requires leaders of the future to find a balance between endorsing a tech-infused efficiency model as the new way of working, and promoting awareness that creativity, empathy and ethical judgments ultimately matter most when assessing the value created by employing algorithms. To achieve this balance requires continuous education and training. Indeed, leaders of tomorrow will have to participate in continuous education in two ways.[212]

Education should first address employees on the topic of new technology. Too often digital transformations fail because of people's lack of knowledge. This ignorance leads to a lack of understanding in how it can be used to drive performance of the organization. It is therefore imperative that organizations train and continuously update their workforce so that they have a basic understanding of, for example, coding and its potential use for task execution. The *Wall Street Journal* reported that Amazon plans to spend $700m over the next six years to train 100,000 of its workforce in new technology skills.[213] Similarly, Microsoft has built the AI Business School to share knowledge and insights from top executives and thought leaders on how to strategically use AI in organizations.[214] It is this tech savviness that can make leaders more effective in employing algorithms in the most optimal ways. At the same time, it enables human employees to understand why this new (non-human) employee is needed.

A second type of education should promote the human skills considered necessary for future leaders. Indeed, we do not want leaders to get so wrapped up in the most sophisticated technological advancements that they lose sight of building a vision that has the human identity at its core. Our workforce will therefore have to be educated continuously in the emotional and creative skills required to build a tech-driven organization where questions around ethics, privacy and innovation for humankind are frequently shared and discussed.

Humanity in AI as a guiding tool

It is important to emphasize that the need for continuous education brings with it the question of what it is that the leaders of tomorrow need to know. Indeed, the two-fold approach to continuous education makes clear that organizations empowering algorithms in their search for efficiency do not require leadership thinking *dominated* by technology insights. Rather, a basic understanding of new technology will need to be complemented more than ever with insights from other, more humane fields, like philosophy and psychology. After all, even in a tech-dominated business world, organizations are still more likely to succeed if they act in a more, as opposed to less, human manner.

Consider the following assertion made by the intellectual fathers of AI, that AI is not developed with the purpose of replacing the human race – and thereby reversing the power dynamics – in a society that is becoming increasingly automated. Instead, it aims to contribute to the optimization and well-being of a human society defined by the unique values that make it human. The following passage from a 1960 article by Norbert Wiener, the founder of cybernetics, is particularly compelling in this respect: "If we use, to achieve our purposes, a mechanical agency with whose operation we cannot efficiently interfere once we have started it because the action is so fast and irrevocable that we have not the data to intervene before the action is complete, then we better be quite sure that the purpose put into the machine is the purpose which we really desire and not merely a colorful imitation of it."[215]

With this peculiar challenge in mind, I would like to return to the story that I told you earlier, about my executive students asking whether soft skills will have a place in the leadership of tomorrow. As you may recall, many of them were worried about their own position and were contemplating devoting all their energy and time to becoming more skilled in coding. What is the truth here? Is it a valid concern and should it be addressed?

Yes, it should be addressed, and it is fine that leaders in organizations devote more resources to learning programming. However, it is not fine for leaders to think that the leadership skills of yesterday will no longer be required tomorrow. It is not alright if leaders today are pushed into thinking that our soft skills will have to be replaced with our newly-acquired tech skills. In fact, this line of thinking cannot be more wrong. Rather than leaders becoming more machine in their thinking, leaders should endeavor to become even more human!

As I have pointed out in this chapter, understanding the workings and sensitivities of the new technology is not an end in itself. Indeed, leaders today should not be asked to transform themselves into data analysts. The skill of being tech savvy is required because it represents a means of becoming more effective in augmenting the performance of the organization, but always from a human perspective. As such, the education of our leaders should be based on an understanding of new technology, but elevated by the skill of critical thinking and enhanced with reflection on what this technology means for our human identity.

Other voices utter the same idea. For example, Peter Thiel (an American entrepreneur and venture capitalist) announced that "People are spending way too much time thinking about climate change, and way too little thinking about AI." Equally, the late Stephen Hawking (Cambridge University professor), warned in *The Independent* that success in our search for AI domination, while it would be "the biggest event in human history," might very well "also be the last, unless we learn to avoid the risks."

Even Bill Gates has publicly admitted of his disquiet, speaking of his inability to "understand why some people are not concerned." Whether these concerns, uttered by the famous, are true or not, they are shared by many more. For example, in November 2018, *The Guardian* published an article titled, 'The truth about killer robots,' and a month later, *The Economist* wrote: "There are no killer robots yet – but regulators must respond to AI in 2019."[216,217] What these examples make clear, is that the education of our future leaders needs to include a strong emphasis on thinking about the consequences that algorithms in our organizations and society bring to our own human identity.

Tolerance for imperfection

By prioritizing our human identity, leaders of tomorrow will be able to drive algorithm-based transformations in ways that enable us to lead the development of technology rather than being led by technology itself. One key aspect of a humane society is the fact that we are able to be compassionate and forgive mistakes. In other words, we can be tolerant of imperfect behavior while we search for progress. Indeed, as the famous French writer and philosopher Voltaire once said: "What is tolerance? It is a necessary consequence of humanity. We are all fallible, let us then pardon each other's follies. This is the first principle of natural right."

Algorithms and deep learning techniques are focused on being more accurate and effective than ever before. In other words, a new technology focus brings with it a focus on perfection. If we allow this kind of thinking to dominate and take the place of leadership, then it is a legitimate concern that we may grow into organizations and societies that do not respect personal freedom. In fact, a shift towards perfection and consequently a rejection of being tolerant to human failures, which would slowly remove humanity from the algorithm equation, may already be happening.

Think, for example, about the use of facial recognition. China is currently using 170m cameras empowered by AI to fight crime and increase general security. Obviously, these are good reasons to use this kind of technology. But, think about it, if we adopt this facial recognition technology without spending at least some time pondering what it does to human values, such as our right of privacy and human freedom, then we may quickly develop a society where opposition against the new technology will no longer be tolerated. If this is the case, submission to machine will be total and the only way forward will then be to follow the logic of the machine advocating the use of complete transparency without the opportunity to challenge.

However, how much humanity does such a system represent? It is very likely that any human desire to avoid being screened in its entirety will then only elicit suspicion, because why oppose infringement of personal freedom if you have nothing to hide? Opposition should only happen if you have something to hide. Of course, if such kinds of thinking become the default, then we already have moved into a society that does not allow humans to make their own choices. After all, from the perspective of the *perfect* society as orchestrated by the *perfect* machine, human choices are imperfect and prone to failure.

In fact, under such a machine-driven regime, allowing individual freedom of choice only brings the risk of imperfection and therefore represents a threat to the dream of constructing the perfect society system. Hence, the use of algorithms on such a large and intimate scale may well be leading to a less humane society. It is in light of these concerns that we must view the recent decision of San Francisco to ban facial recognition, or the comment of Brad Smith, president of Microsoft, that it would be best for us to take a principled approach (driven by values like fairness, non-discrimination, notice and consent) toward the use and development of facial-recognition technology.[218]

Important in this challenge, of leaders staying close to the mission of ensuring humanity in our technological pursuit, is the realization that the task of automation requires the building of moral communities. The moral communities I talk about represent the ethical values that we, as humans, see as crucial to our identity. They represent the ethical values that we would like to see pursued through the application of new technology.

It cannot be that by introducing the new technology, we create a work culture where moral obligations and responsibilities – which were considered normal in the past – are pushed aside (and ultimately forgotten) in the organization of tomorrow. For example, replacing nurses with care robots may be effective in responding to labor shortages in hospitals, but, at the same time, if this new technological innovation is not led by leaders applying a humane perspective, we may forget that one important human value that needs to remain is to take care of each other. If technological revolutions lead to a shallow approach to humanity, innovations like care robots may ultimately lead to an increase in social isolation among humans. And that should not be an outcome that any human leader would wish to see happen.

Conclusion

I N   L I G H T   O F   the human race's ambition to evolve by means of technological innovation, we have to be careful not to harm ourselves by losing the one thing that defines us: our human identity. If this happens, we have no one to blame except ourselves. And the reason is simple.

We are developing the idea that growth in efficiency is the best way to achieve contributions to the public good. And because of this desire to optimize, we run the risk of having to submit to the machine and, in the process, evaluate ourselves with the same criteria we used for machines. If this continues, the road forward will be one where humans join machines and ultimately become machines (or at least those who meet the requested criteria will). As a result, humanity is taken out of the equation. Is this a realistic point of view? Can humans feel better in a machine-driven world than in one dictated by the human race?

If we use the science fiction world as a guide, then it could well be the case. Take, for example, the 2009 movie *Avatar*, directed by James Cameron. In this movie, a reality is painted where humans can live in a virtual world, yet still partake in emotional and physical experiences. By becoming an avatar, the idea is formed of humans being able to enter the world of technology and become an actual part of it. What is interesting in movies depicting such a reality is that it shows that humans can quickly develop a kind of addiction to such an alternate life and see it as rewarding. Once the reward centers are activated in our brain, it becomes addictive and we want more of it. We want *more* machine.

Consider the 2018 movie *Oasis*, which depicts a society in 2045 where people can take the shape of any character in a virtual world called the Oasis. In the Oasis, people can live their fantasies, which is not a problem as long as we realize that the virtual world is different from the human one in which we actually live. This is, however, something the main character

Wade Watts (played by actor Tye Sheridan) fails to do, as he falls in love with the virtual character Art3mis (played by actress Olivia Cooke). By not being able to distinguish between the worlds and preferring to experience the virtual world over the actual one, the main character becomes addicted to spending more and more time in the Oasis.

Granted, these movies are simply fiction and as such can be considered unrealistic and not relevant to the technology challenges that we are facing today. But, at the same time, they do provide us with valuable advice, since they outline how quickly our human desire to progress at any cost can escalate quickly into submission to a technology system that strips away our true human identity.

Moreover, living a virtual life may not be a fantasy for that much longer. For example, Neuralink, a start-up founded by Elon Musk, is currently working on developing a brain-machine interface where human and AI can meet. On the surface, this does not need to be a problem, as long as AI is only used to augment human capabilities and the reality established is human. The point I want to emphasize here, however, is that humans need to have a strong moral compass in their search to continuously improve themselves with new technology. Without any ethical awareness of how we want to use algorithms, and for what purpose, we may run the risk of becoming blinded by the unlimited technological opportunities available to us. As a result, we may lose the unique human features that shape and define our societies and organizations. And if this is to happen, at best, humans will follow machines, but at worst, we may, as a species, cease to exist.

Guidance is needed before we embrace the potential of algorithms in our workplace and use them to serve humanity. That ambition in itself requires a leader that understands, feels and recognizes human experience as an opportunity, not a limitation. All of this leads to the conclusion that the leadership of the future is likely to remain human.

Endnotes

Chapter 1

1   Reeves, M. (2015). 'Algorithms Can Make Your Organization Self-Tuning.' *Harvard Business Review*. May 13. Retrieved from: https://hbr.org/2015/05/algorithms-can-make-your-organization-self-tuning

2   Andrews, L. (2019). 'Public administration, public leadership and the construction of public value in the age of algorithm and big data.' *Public Administration*, 97(2), 296-310.

3   Fountaine, T., McCarthy, B., & Saleh, T. (2019). 'Building the AI-powered Organization.' *Harvard Business Review*, July-August, 2-13.

4   Lehnis, M. (2018). 'Can we trust AI if we don't know how it works?' Retrieved from https://www.bbc.com/news/business-44466213

5   Accenture (2017). 'AI as the new UI – Accenture Tech Vision.' Retrieved from: https://www.accenture.com/t20171005T065832Z__w__/us-en/_acnmedia/Accenture/next-gen-4/tech-vision-2017/pdf/Accenture-TV17-Trend-1.pdf

6   Accenture (2018). 'Realizing the full value of AI.' Retrieved from: https://www.accenture.com/_acnmedia/pdf-77/accenture-workforce-banking-survey-report

7   Chui, M., Henke, M., Miremadi, M. (2018). 'Most of AI's Business Uses Will Be in Two Areas.' *Harvard Business Review*. July 20. Retrieved from: https://hbr.org/2018/07/most-of-ais-business-uses-will-be-in-two-areas

8   McKinsey (2018). 'Notes from the AI frontier: Applications and value of deep learning.' Retrieved from: https://www.mckinsey.com/featured-insights/artificial-intelligence/notes-from-the-ai-frontier-applications-and-value-of-deep-learning

9   Bloomberg (2018, January 15th). 'Alibaba's AI Outguns Humans in Reading Test.' Retrieved from https://www.bloomberg.com/news/articles/2018-01-15/alibaba-s-ai-outgunned-humans-in-key-stanford-reading-test

10   Gee, K. (2017). 'In Unilever's Radical Hiring Experiment, Resumes Are Out, Algorithms Are In.' *The Wall Street Journal*. Retrieved from https://www.wsj.com/articles/in-unilevers-radical-hiring-experiment-resumes-are-out-algorithms-are-in-1498478400

11   Glaser, V. (2014). 'Enchanted Algorithms: How Organizations Use Algorithms to Automate Decision-Making Routines.' *Academy of Management Proceedings*, 2014(1), 12938.

12   Hoffman, M., Kahn, L.B., & Li, D. (2017). 'Discretion in hiring.' *NBER Working Paper* No. 21709. Retrieved from: https://www.nber.org/papers/w21709?sy=709

13   Son, H. (2015). 'JP Morgan algorithm knows you're a rogue employee before you do.' (8 April 2015). Retrieved from: https://www.bloomberg.com/news/articles/2015-04-08/jpmorgan-algorithm-knows-you-re-a-rogue-employee-before-you-do.

14   Hoffman, M., Kahn, L.B., & Li, D. (2017). 'Discretion in hiring.' *NBER Working Paper* No. 21709. Retrieved from: https://www.nber.org/papers/w21709?sy=709

15   Fethi, M.D., & Fotios, P. (2010). 'Assessing bank efficiency and performance with operational research and artificial intelligence techniques: A survey.' *European Journal of Operational Research*, 204(2), 189-198.

16   Greer, S., Lodge, G., Mazzini, J., & Yanagawa, E. (2018). 'Global Tech spending forecast: Banking edition.' 20 March 2018. Retrieved from: https://www.celent.com/insights/929209647

17   Paterl, V.L., Shortliffe, E.H., Stefanelli, M., Szolovits, O.P., Berthold, M.R., & Abu-Hanna, A. (2009). 'The coming age of artificial intelligence in medicine.' *Artificial Intelligence in Medicine*, 46(1), 5-17.

18   Leachman, S.A., & Merlino, G. (2017). 'The final frontier in cancer diagnosis.' *Nature*, 542, 36.

19   Bennett, C.C., & Hauer, K. (2013). 'Artificial intelligence framework for simulating clinical decision-making: A Markov decision process approach.' *Artificial Intelligence in Medicine*, 57(1), 9-19.

20   Wang, D., Khosla, A., Gargeya, R., Irshad, H., & Beck, A.H. (2016). 'Deep learning for identifying metastatic breast cancer.' arXiv, preprint arXiv:1606.05718. Copy at http://j.mp/2o6FejM

21   Dawes, R. M., (1979). 'The robust beauty of improper linear models in decision making.' *American Psychologist*, 34(7), 571-582.

22   Dawes, R. M., Faust, D., & Meehl, P. E. (1989). 'Clinical versus Actuarial Judgment.' *Heuristics and Biases*, 716-729.

23   Kleinmuntz, D. N., & Schkade, D. A. (1993). 'Information displays and decision processes.' *Psychological Science*, 4(4), 221-227.

24   Adams, I.D., Chan, M., Clifford, P.C., et al. (1986). 'Computer aided diagnosis of acute abdominal pain: A multicentre study.' *British Medical Journal*, 2093, 800-804.

25   Beck, A. H., Sangoi, A. R., Leung, S., Marinelli, R. J., Nielsen, T. O., Van De Vijver, M. J., & Koller, D. (2011). 'Systematic analysis of breast cancer morphology uncovers stromal features associated with survival.' *Science translational medicine*, 3(108), doi: 108ra113-108ra113

26   Grove, W. M., Zald, D. H., Lebow, B. S., Snitz, B. E., & Nelson, C. (2000). 'Clinical versus mechanical prediction: A meta-analysis.' *Psychological Assessment*, 12(1), 19-30.

27   Maidens, J., & Slamon, N.B. (2018). Abstract12591: 'Artificial intelligence detects pediatric heart murmurs with cardiologist-level accuracy.' *Circulation*, 138 (suppl_1).

28   Highhouse, S. (2008). 'Stubborn Reliance on Intuition and Subjectivity in Employee Selection.' *Industrial and Organizational Psychology*, 1 (3), 333-342.

29   Schweitzer, M.E., & Cachon, G.P. (2000). 'Decision bias in the newsvendor problem with a known demand distribution: Experimental evidence.' *Management Science*, 46(3), 404-420.

30   Frey, C. B., & Osborne, M. A. (2017). 'The future of employment: how susceptible are jobs to computerisation?' *Technological Forecasting and Social Change*, 114, 254-280.

31   Accenture (2017). 'The promise of Artificial Intelligence: Redefining management in the workforce of the future.' Retrieved from: https://www.accenture.com/no-en/insight-promise-artificial-intelligence

32   PwC (2019). 'AI Predictions: Six AI priorities you can't afford to ignore.' Retrieved from: https://www.pwc.com/us/en/services/consulting/library/artificial-intelligence-predictions-2019?WT.mc_id=CT13-PL1300-DM2-TR1-LS4-ND30-TTA5-CN_ai2019-ai19-digpul-1&eq=CT13-PL1300-DM2-CN_ai2019-ai19-digpul-1

33   Salesforce Research (2019). 'State of Service.' Insights and trends from over 3,500 service leaders and agents worldwide. Retrieved from: https://www.salesforce.com/blog/2019/03/customer-service-trends.html

34   Hoffman, P. (1986). 'The Unity of Descartes' Man,' *The Philosophical Review* 95, 339-369.

35   Google Duplex (2018). https://www.youtube.com/watch?v=D5VN 56jQMWM

Chapter 2

36   Naqvi, A. (2017). 'Responding to the will of the machine: Leadership in the age of artificial intelligence.' *Journal of Economics Bibliography*, 4(3), 244-250.

37   Gamson, W.A., & Scotch, N.A. (1964). 'Scapegoating in baseball.' *American Journal of Sociology*, 70, 69-72.

38   Pfeffer, J., & Salancik, G.R. (1978). 'The external control of organizations: A resource dependence perspective.' New York: Harper & Row Publishers.

39   Pfeffer, J. (1977). 'The ambiguity of leadership.' *Academy of Management Review*, 2, 104-112.

40   MacCrory, F., Westerman, G., Alhammadi, Y., & Brynjolfsson, E. (2014). 'Racing with and against the machine: Changes in occupational skill composition in an era of rapid technological advance.' In Proceedings of the 35th International Conference on Information Systems (pp. 295–311). Red Hook, NY: Curran Associates Inc.

41   von Krogh, G. (2018). 'Artificial intelligence in organizations: New opportunities for phenomenon-based theorizing.' *Academy of Management Discoveries*, 4(4), 404-409.

42   Parry, K., Cohen, M., & Bhattacharya, S. (2016). 'Rise of the machines: A critical consideration of automated leadership decision making in organizations.' *Group & Organization Management*, 41(5), 571-594.

43   Lindebaum, D., Vesa, M., & den Hond, F. (in press). 'Insights from the machine stops to better understand rational assumptions in algorithmic decision-making and its implications for organizations.' *Academy of Management Review*.

44   Derrick, D.C., & Elson, J.S. (2019). 'Exploring automated leadership and agent interaction modalities.' Proceedings of the 52nd Hawaii International Conference on System Sciences, 207-216.

45 SAS (2018). 'Becoming a data-driven organization.' https://analyticsconsultores.com.mx/wp-content/uploads/2019/03/Becoming-a-data-driven-organization-Citizen-Data-Scientist-SAS-2018.pdf

46 Copeland, R., & Hope, B. (2016). 'The world's largest hedge fund is building an algorithmic model from its employees' brains.' Retrieved from https://www.wsj.com/articles/the-worlds-largest-hedge-fund-is-building-an-algorithmic-model-of-its-founders-brain-1482423694 on 31 October 2018.

47 Nelson, J. (2019). 'AI in the boardroom – Fantasy or reality?' March 26. Retrieved from http://www.mondaq.com/x/792746/new+technology/AI+In+The+Boardroom+Fantasy+Or+Reality

48 Libert, B., Beck, M., & Bonchek, M. (2017). 'AI in the boardroom: The next realm of corporate governance.' February 21. Retrieved from https://sloanreview.mit.edu/article/ai-in-the-boardroom-the-next-realm-of-corporate-governance/

49 Amazon (2019). https://www.businessinsider.sg/amazon-system-automatically-fires-warehouse-workers-time-off-task-2019-4/?r=US&IR=T

50 Acemoglu, D., & Restrepo, P. (2019). 'Robots and jobs: Evidence from US labor markets.' *Journal of Political Economy*. Accepted August 1.

51 IBM (2019). 'Unplug from the Past: 19th Global C-Suite Study,' IBM Institute for Business Value, 2018, https://www.ibm.com/downloads/cas/D2KEJQRO

52 LinkedIn (2019). 'The Rise of HR Analytics,' 2018, https://business.linkedin.com/content/dam/me/business/en-us/talent-solutions/talent-intelligence/workforce/pdfs/Final_v2_NAMER_Riseof-Analytics-Report.pdf.

Chapter 3

53 Drucker, P. (1967). 'The manager and the moron.' *McKinsey Quarterly*, 4. mckinsey.com

54 Ikujiro, N., & Hirotaka, T. (2011). 'The wise leader.' *Harvard Business Review*, May, 89(5), 58-67.

55 Bigman, Y. E., & Gray, K. (2018). 'People are averse to machines making moral decisions.' *Cognition*, 181, 21-34.

56 Gray, H.M., Gray, K., & Wegner, D.M. (2007). 'Dimensions of mind perception.' *Science*, 315(5812), 619.

57   Hogan, R., & Kaiser, R. B. (2005). 'What we know about leadership.' *Review of General Psychology*, 9, 169.

58   Finkelstein, S., Cannella, S.F.B., & Hambrick, D.C. (2009). 'Strategic leadership: Theory and research on executives, top management teams, and boards.' Oxford University Press: New York.

59   Messick, D. M., & Bazerman, M. (1996). 'Ethical leadership and the psychology of decision making.' *Sloan Management Review*, 37, 9-22.

60   Logg, J., Minson, J.A., & Moore, D.A. (2019). 'Algorithm Appreciation: People Prefer Algorithmic to Human Judgment.' *Organizational Behavior and Human Decision Processes*, 151, 90-103.

61   Granulo, A., Fuchs C., & Puntoni, S. (2019). 'Psychological reactions to human versus robotic job replacement.' *Nature Human Behavior*, 3, 1062-1069.

62   Gartner (2018). 'Gartner says 25% of customer service operations will use virtual customer assistants by 2020.' Retrieved from: https://www.gartner.com/en/newsroom/press-releases/2018-02-19-gartner-says-25-percent-of-customer-service-operations-will-use-virtual-customer-assistants-by-2020

63   Capgemini Research Institute (2018). 'Conversational commerce. Why consumers are embracing voice assistants in their lives.' Retrieved from: https://www.capgemini.com/resources/conversational-commerce-dti-report/

64   Curchod, C., Patriotta, G., & Cohen, L. (in press). 'Working for an algorithm: power asymmetries and agency in online work settings.' *Administrative Science Quarterly*.

65   Shamir, B. (2007). 'From passive recipients to active co-producers: followers' role in the leadership process.' In B. Shamir, R. Pillai, & Bligh, M.C. (Eds.), Follower-centered perspectives on leadership: A tribute to the memory of James R. Meindl. Greenwich, CT: Information Age Publishing.

66   Davenport, T.H., & Bean, R. (2018). 'Big Companies Are Embracing Analytics, But Most Still Don't Have a Data-Driven Culture.' *Harvard Business Review*, 15 February. Retrieved from: https://hbr.org/2018/02/big-companies-are-embracing-analytics-but-most-still-dont-have-a-data-driven-culture

67   Castelvechi, D. (2016). 'The black box of AI.' *Nature*, 538, 20-23.

68   Zeng, Z., Miao, C., Leung, C. & Chin, J.J. (2018). 'Building more explainable Artificial Intelligence with argumentation.' *Association for the Advancement of Artificial Intelligence*, 8044-8045.

69   Frick, W. (2015). 'Here's why people trust human judgment over algorithms.' *Harvard Business Review*, February 27. Retrieved from: https://hbr.org/2015/02/heres-why-people-trust-human-judgment-over-algorithms

70   Diab, D. L., Pui, S. Y., Yankelevich, M., & Highhouse, S. (2011). 'Lay perceptions of selection decision aids in US and non-US samples.' *International Journal of Selection and Assessment*, 19(2), 209-216.

71   Eastwood, J., Snook, B., & Luther, K. (2012). 'What people want from their professionals: Attitudes toward decision-making strategies.' *Journal of Behavioral Decision Making*, 25(5), 458-468.

72   Önkal, D., Goodwin, P., Thomson, M., Gönül, S., & Pollock, A. (2009). 'The relative influence of advice from human experts and statistical methods on forecast adjustments.' *Journal of Behavioral Decision Making*, 22(4), 390-409.

73   Promberger, M., & Baron, J. (2006). 'Do patients trust computers?' *Journal of Behavioral Decision Making*, 19(5), 455-468.

74   Shaffer, V.A., Probst, C.A., Merkle, E.C., Arkes, H.R. & Medow, M.A. (2013). 'Why do patients derogate physicians who use a computer-based diagnostic support system?' *Medical Decision Making*, 33(1), 108-118.

75   Dietvorst, B. J., Simmons, J. P., & Massey, C. (2015). 'Algorithm aversion: People erroneously avoid algorithms after seeing them err.' *Journal of Experimental Psychology: General*, 144(1), 114-126.

76   Dimitrov, A. (2018). 'The digital age leadership: A transhumanistic perspective.' *Journal of Leadership Studies*, 12(3), 79–81.

77   Grove, W. M., & Meehl, P. E. (1996). 'Comparative efficiency of informal (subjective, impressionistic) and formal (mechanical, algorithmic) prediction procedures: The clinical–statistical controversy.' *Psychology, Public Policy, and Law*, 2(2), 293.

Chapter 4

78   Kotter, J.P. (2013). 'Management is (still) not leadership,' *Harvard Business Review*, 9 January. Retrieved from: https://hbr.org/2013/01/management-is-still-not-leadership

79   Hamel, G., & Zanini, M. (2018). 'Busting bureaucracy.' Blog retrieved from http://www.garyhamel.com/blog/busting-bureaucracy

80   Saval, N. (2014). 'Cubed: A secret history of the workplace.' New York: Doubleday.

81   Kotter, J.P. (1990). 'Force for change: How leadership differs from management.' The Free Press.

82   Kotter, J.P. (1995). 'What leaders really do.' In J.T. Wren (Ed.), *The Leaders Companion* (pp. 114-123). The Free Press.

83   Awamleh, R., & Gardner, W. L. (1999). 'Perceptions of leader charisma and effectiveness: The effects of vision content, delivery, and organizational performance.' *The Leadership Quarterly*, 10, 345–373.

84   Kotterman, J. (2006). 'Leadership versus management: What's the difference?' *The Journal for Quality and Participation*, 29(2), 13-17.

85   Kotter, J.P. (1990). 'Force for change: How leadership differs from management.' The Free Press.

86   Kotterman, J. (2006). 'Leadership versus management: What's the difference?' *The Journal for Quality and Participation*, 29(2), 13-17.

87   Yukl, G. (1998). 'Leadership in organizations.' Upper Saddle River, NJ: Prentice Hall.

88   Bass, B.M. (2000). 'The future of leadership in learning organizations.' *Journal of Leadership & Organizational Studies*, 7(3), 18-40.

Chapter 5

89   Tarnoff, B. (2017). 'Silicon Valley siphons our data like oil. But the deepest drilling has just begun.' *The Guardian*. Retrieved from: https://www.theguardian.com/world/2017/aug/23/silicon-valley-big-data-extraction-amazon-whole-foods-facebook

90   Thorp, J. (2012). 'Big data is not the new oil.' *Harvard Business Review*. November 30. Retrieved from: https://hbr.org/2012/11/data-humans-and-the-new-oil

91   Lapuschkin, S., Wäldchen, S., Binder, A., Montavon, G., Samek, W., & Mueller, K.-R. (2019). 'Unmasking clever Hans predictors and assessing what machines really learn.' *Nature Communications*, 10, 1096.

92   Editorial (2017). 'How does the brain work?' *Neuron*, 94(5), 933.

93   Goldhill, O., (2015). 'Algorithms make better hiring decisions than humans.' Retrieved from: https://qz.com/561206/algorithms-make-better-hiring-decisions-than-humans/

94   Fly, A. (2019). 'The skills leaders need to survive in the age of AI,' https://www.techradar.com/sg/news/the-skills-leaders-need-to-survive-in-the-age-of-ai)

95   IBM (2018). 'Power your candidate experience with AI.' Retrieved from: https://newsroom.ibm.com/IBM-watson?item=30401 (also, Leight-Deobald et al., (in press). 'The challenges of algorithm-based HR decision-making for personal integrity.' *Journal of Business Ethics*.)

96   Bonczek, R.H., Holsapple, C.W., & Whinston, A.B. (1979). 'Computer-based support of organizational decision making.' *Decision Sciences*, 10(2), 268-291.

97   Courtney, J.F. (2001). 'Decision making and knowledge management in inquiring organizations: Toward a new decision-making paradigm for DSS.' *Decision Support Systems*, 31(1), 17-38.

98   Gigerenzer, G., & Gaissmaier, W. (2011). 'Heuristic Decision Making.' *Annual Review of Psychology*, 62, 451-482.

99   Huber, G. (1990). 'A theory of the effects of advanced information technologies on organizational design, intelligence and decision making,' *Academy of Management Review*, 15(1), 47-71.

100 Pomerol, J.-C. (1997). 'Artificial intelligence and human decision making.' *European Journal of Operational Research*, 99(1), 3-25.

101 Russel, S.J., & Norvig, P. (2016). 'Artificial intelligence: A modern approach.' Pearson Education Limited.

102 Rosenblat, A., Kneese, T., & Boyd, D. (2014). 'Workplace surveillance.' *Data & Society Working Paper*. New York: Data & Society Research Institute.

103 Volini, E., Schwartz, J., Roy, I., Hauptmann, M., Van Durme, Y., Denny, B., & Bersin, J. (2019). 'Organizational performance: It's a team sport.' Deloitte report, 2019 Global Human Capital Trends. April 11. Retrieved from: https://trendsapp.deloitte.com/reports/2019/global-human-capital-trends/organizational-performance.html

104 De Cremer, D., McGuire, J., Naryanan, J., Tang, P., & Mai, M. K. (2020). 'How fair and trustworthy automated assessment systems are: it depends on you speaking up and your supervisor's humility.' Working paper NUS Business School.

105 Kelly, K. (2016). 'The inevitable: Understanding the 12 technological forces that will shape our future.' Viking Press.

Chapter 6

106 Geraerts, E. (2019). 'Authentieke Intelligentie: Waarom mensen altijd winnen van computers.' Prometheus.

107 Avolio, B.J., Walumbwa, F.O., & Weber, T.J. (2009). 'Leadership: Current theories, research and future directions.' *Annual Review of Psychology*, 60, 421-449.

108 Hazy, T.E., Frank, M.J., & O' Reilly, R.C. (2007). 'Towards an executive without a homunculus: computational models of the prefrontal cortex/basal ganglia system.' *Philosophical Transactions of the Royal Society* B, 362(1485).

109 Uhl-Bien, M., Marion, R., McKelvey, B. (2007). 'Complexity leadership theory: Shifting leadership from the industrial age to the knowledge era.' *The Leadership Quarterly*, 18(4), 298-318.

110 De Cremer, D. (2013). 'The proactive leader: How to overcome procrastination and be a bold decision-maker.' Palgrave MacMillan.

111 Jarrahi, M. H. (2018). 'Artificial intelligence and the future of work: Human-AI symbiosis in organizational decision making.' *Business Horizons*, 61(4), 577-586.

112 Malone, T.W. (2018). 'How human-computer 'Superminds' are redefining the future of work.' *Sloan Management Review*, 59(4), 34-41.

113 De Cremer, D., McGuire, J., Hesselbarth, Y., & Mai, M. (2019). 'Can algorithms help us decide who to trust?' *Harvard Business Review*. 6 June. Retrieved from: https://hbr.org/2019/06/can-algorithms-help-us-decide-who-to-trust

114 Bigman, Y. E., & Gray, K. (2018). 'People are averse to machines making moral decisions.' *Cognition*, 181, 21-34.

115 Gray, H.M., Gray, K., & Wegner, D.M. (2007). 'Dimensions of mind perception.' *Science*, 315(5812), 619.

116 Fiske, S.T., Cuddy, A.J.C., & Glick, P. (2007). 'Universal dimensions of social cognition: warmth and competence.' *Trends in Cognitive Science*, 11(2), 77-83.

117 Gray, K., Jenkins, A.C., Heberlein, A.S., & Wegner, D.M. (2011). 'Distortions of mind perception in psychopathology.' Proceedings of the National Academy of Sciences of the United States of America, 108(2), 477-479.

118 Haslam, N. (2006). 'Dehumanization: An integrative review.' *Personality and Social Psychology Review*, 10(3), 252-264.

119 Knobe, J., & Prinz, J. (2008). 'Intuitions about consciousness: Experimental studies.' *Phenomenology and the Cognitive Sciences*, 7(1), 67-83.

120 Jack, A.I., & Robbins, P. (2012). 'The phenomenal stance revisited.' *Review of Philosophy and Psychology*, 3(3), 383-403.

121 De Cremer, D., McGuire, J., Hesselbarth, Y., & Mai, M. (2019). 'Can algorithms help us decide who to trust?' *Harvard Business Review*. 6 June. Retrieved from: https://hbr.org/2019/06/can-algorithms-help-us-decide-who-to-trust

122 De Cremer, D. (2003). 'How self-conception may lead to inequality: An experimental investigation of the impact of hierarchical roles on the equality-rule when allocating organizational resources.' *Group and Organization Management*, 28(2), 282-302.

123 Kaplan, A., & Haenlein, M. (in press). 'Rulers of the world, unite! The challenges and opportunities of artificial intelligence.' *Business Horizons*.

124 Ready, D.A. (2019). 'In praise of the incurably curious leader.' July 2018. Retrieved from: https://sloanreview.mit.edu/article/in-praise-of-the-incurably-curious-leader/

125 Pelaprat, E. & Cole, M. (2011). 'Minding the gap: Imagination, creativity and human cognition.' *Integrative Psychological and Behavioral Science*, 45, 397-418.

126 Talat, U. & Chang, K. (2017). 'Employee imagination and implications for entrepreneurs.' *Journal of Chinese Human Resource Management*, 8(2), 129-152.

127 Zhou, J. & Hoever, I.J. (2014). 'Research on workplace creativity.' *Annual Review of Organizational Psychology and Organizational Behavior*, 1, 333-359.

128 Amabile, T.M. (1983). 'The social psychology of creativity: A componential conceptualization.' *Journal of Personality and Social Psychology*, 45(2), 357-376.

129 Kelley, S. (2019). 'This physicist is trying to make sense of the brain's tangled networks.' April 11. Retrieved from: https://www.sciencemag.org/news/2019/04/physicist-trying-make-sense-brain-s-tangled-networks

130 Nijstad, B.A., De Dreu, C.K.W., Rietzschel, E.F., & Baas, M. (2010). 'The dual pathway to creativity model: Creative ideation as a function of flexibility and persistence.' *European Review of Social Psychology*, 21, 34-77.

131 De Cremer, D. (2019). 'Leading Artificial Intelligence at work: A matter of facilitating human-algorithm co-creation.' *Journal of Leadership Studies*, 13(1), 81-83.

132 Goleman, D. (2011). 'Leadership: The power of emotional intelligence.' *More than Sound* (1st edition).

133 Hasan, A. (2019). 'Demand for emotional intelligence skills soars six folds.' November 5. Retrieved from: https://www.peoplemattersglobal.com/news/employee-assistance-programs/demand-for-emotional-intelligence-skills-soars-six-folds-23636

134 Law, K.S., Wong, C.-S., Huang, G.-H., & Li, X. (2008). 'The effects of emotional intelligence on job performance and life satisfaction for the research and development scientists in China.' *Asia Pacific Journal of Management*, 25, 51-69.

135 Huang, M.-H., Rust, R., & Maksimovic, V. (2019). 'The feeling economy: Managing in the next generation of Artificial Intelligence (AI).' *California Management Review*, 61(4), 43-65.

136 Jago, A.S. (2019). 'Algorithms and authenticity.' *Academy of Management Discoveries*, 5, 38-56.

137 Bigman, Y.E. & Gray, K. (2018). 'People are aversive to machines making moral decisions.' *Cognition*, 181, 21-34.

138 Jago, A.S. (2019). 'Algorithms and authenticity.' *Academy of Management Discoveries*, 5, 38-56.

139 Reynolds, S.J. (2006). 'Moral awareness and ethical predispositions: Investigating the role of individual differences in the recognition of moral issues.' *Journal of Applied Psychology*, 91(1), 233-243.

140 Treviño, L.K., Weaver, G.R., & Reynolds, S.J. (2006). 'Behavioral ethics in organizations: A review.' *Journal of Management*, 32(6), 991-1022.

141 Rest, J.R. (1986). 'Moral development: Advances in research and theory.' Praeger: New York.

142 Brown, M.E., Treviño, L.K, & Harrison, D.A. (2005). 'Ethical leadership: A social learning perspective for construct development and testing.' *Organizational Behavior and Human Decision Processes*, 97(2), 117-134.

143 Davenport, (2019). 'What does an AI ethicist do?' June 24. Retrieved from: https://sloanreview.mit.edu/article/what-does-an-ai-ethicist-do/

144 Fisher, B. (2019). 'Top 5 hires companies need to succeed in 2019.' https://info.kpmg.us/news-perspectives/technology-innovation/top-5-ai-hires-companies-need-to-succeed-in-2019.html

145 Werber, C. (2019). 'The five most important new jobs in AI, according to KPMG.' January 8. Retrieved from: https://qz.com/work/1517594/the-five-most-important-new-ai-jobs-according-to-kpmg/

Chapter 7

146 Parry, K., & Cohen, M. (2016). 'Rise of the machines: A critical consideration of automated leadership decision making in organizations.' *Group and Organization Management*, 41(5), 571-594.

147 von Krogh, G. (2018). 'Artificial intelligence in organizations: New opportunities for phenomenon-based theorizing.' *Academy of Management Discoveries*, 4(4), 404-409.

148 Diab, D.L., Pui, S.-H., Yankelevich, M., & Highhouse, S. (2011). 'Lay perceptions of selection decision aids in US and Non-US samples.' *International Journal of Selection and Assessment*, 19(2), 209-216.

149 Promberger, M. & Baron, J. (2006). 'Do patients trust computers?' *Journal of Behavioral Decision Making*, 19(5), 455-468.

150 Dietvorst, B. J., Simmons, J. P., & Massey, C. (2015). 'Algorithm aversion: People erroneously avoid algorithms after seeing them err.' *Journal of Experimental Psychology: General*, 144(1), 114-126.

151 Ariely, D. (2009). 'Predictably irrational: The hidden forces that shape our decisions.' HarperCollins.

152 Shaffer, V.A., Probst, A., Merkle, E.C., Arkes, H.R., & Medow, M.A. (2013). 'Why do patients derogate physicians who use a computer-based diagnostic support system?' *Medical Decision Making*, 33(1), 108-118.

153 Gray, H.M., Gray, K., & Wegner, D.M. (2007). 'Dimensions of mind perception.' *Science*, 315(5812), 619.

154 White, R. W. (1959). 'Motivation reconsidered: The concept of competence.' *Psychological Review*, 66(5), 297-333.

155 Bobadilla-Suarez, S., Sunstein, C.R., & Sharot, T. (2017). 'The intrinsic value of choice: The propensity to under-delegate in the face of potential gains and losses.' *Journal of Risk and Uncertainty*, 54, 187-202.

156 De Cremer, D., McGuire, J., Mai, M.K., & Van Hiel, A. (2019). 'Sacrificing to stop autonomous AI.' Working paper NUS Business School.

157 Tyler, T.R. (1997). 'The psychology of legitimacy: A relational perspective on voluntary deference to authorities.' *Personality and Social Psychology Review*, 1(4), 323-345.

158 Berinato, S. (2019). 'Data science and the art of persuasion.' *Harvard Business Review*. Retrieved from: https://hbr.org/2019/01/data-science-and-the-art-of-persuasion

159 Castelvechi, D. (2016). 'The black box of AI.' *Nature*, 538, 20-23.

160 MIT Sloan Management Review and Deloitte (2018). 'Coming of age digitally: Learning, leadership and legacy.' Retrieved from: https://sloanreview.mit.edu/projects/coming-of-age-digitally/?utm_medium=pr&utm_source=release&utm_campaign=dlrpt2018

161 De Cremer, D. & Mancel, P. (2018). 'Leadership is about making others smarter to better serve customers.' *The European Financial Review*, October-November, 57-60.

162 Madhavan, P., & Wiegmann, D.A. (2007). 'Similarities and differences between human-human and human-automation trust: An integrative review.' *Theoretical Issues in Ergonomics Science*, 8(4), 277-301.

163 Shaw, J.C., Wild, E., & Colquitt, J.A. (2003). 'To justify or excuse: A meta-analytic review of the effects of explanations.' *Journal of Applied Psychology*, 88(3), 444-458.

164 Holtz, B. C., & Harold, C. M. (2008). 'When your boss says no! The effects of leadership style and trust on employee reactions to managerial explanations.' *Journal of Occupational and Organizational Psychology*, 81, 777–802.

165 Bies, R. J., Shapiro, D. L., & Cummings, L. L. (1988). 'Casual accounts and managing organizational conflict: Is it enough to say it's not my fault?' *Communication Research*, 15, 381–399.

166 Mansour-Cole, D. M., & Scott, S. G. (1998). 'Hearing it through the grapevine: The influence of source, leader-relations, and legitimacy on survivors' fairness perceptions.' *Personnel Psychology*, 51, 25–54.

167 Bobocel, D. R., & Zdaniuk, A. (2005). 'How can explanations be used to foster organizational justice?' In J. Greenberg & J. A. Colquitt (Eds.), *Handbook of Organizational Justice*. Mahwah, NJ: Lawrence Erlbaum.

168 Dewhurst, M., & Willmott, P. (2014). 'Manager and machine: The new leadership equation.' *McKinsey Quarterly*, 1-8.

169 House, R.J. (1996). 'Path-goal theory of leadership: Lessons, legacy, and a reformulated theory.' *The Leadership Quarterly*, 7(3), 323-352.

Chapter 8

170 Bersin, J. (2016). 'New research shows why focus on teams, not just leaders, is key to business performance.' *Forbes*, March 3. retrieved: https://www.forbes.com/sites/joshbersin/2016/03/03/why-a-focus-on-teams-not-just-leaders-is-the-secret-to-business-performance/#26ead3bb24d5

171 Owana, N. (2018). 'Hyundi exoskeleton aims to cut workers' strains, will be tested in factories.' Retrieved from: https://techxplore.com/news/2018-10-hyundai-exoskeleton-aims-workers-strains.html

172 Wang, D., Khosla, A., Gargeya, R., Irshad, H., & Beck, A.H. (2016). 'Deep learning for identifying metastatic breast cancer.' Copy at http://j.mp/2o6FejM

173 De Cremer, D. (2019). 'On the symphony of AI and humans in the work context.' *The World Financial Review*, September-October, 61-64.

174 Venema, L. (2018). 'Algorithm talk to me.' *Nature Human Behavior*, 2(3), 173-173.

175 Captain, S. (2017). 'Can IBM's Watson Do It All?' *Fast Company*. October 10. Retrieved from: https://www.fastcompany.com/3065339/can-ibms-watson-do-it-all

176 Hinsz, V.B., Tindale, R.S., & Vollrath, D.A. (1997). 'The emerging conceptualization of groups as information processors.' *Psychological Bulletin*, 121(1), 43-64.

177 Dewhurst, M., & Willmott, P. (2014). 'Manager and machine: The new leadership equation.' *McKinsey Quarterly*, 1-8.

178 Hoffman, M., Kahn, L.B., & Li, D. (2017). 'Discretion in hiring.' NBER Working Paper No. 21709. https://www.nber.org/papers/w21709?sy=709

Chapter 9

179 Davenport, T.H., & Bean, R. (2018). 'Big Companies Are Embracing Analytics, But Most Still Don't Have a Data-Driven Culture.' *Harvard Business Review*. February 15. Retrieved from: https://hbr.org/2018/02/big-companies-are-embracing-analytics-but-most-still-dont-have-a-data-driven-culture

180 Bass, B.M. (1985). 'Leadership and Performance Beyond Expectations.' Free Press, New York.

181 Conger, J.A., & Kanungo, R.N. (1987). 'Toward a behavioral theory of charismatic leadership in organizational settings.' *Academy of Management Journal*, 12, 637–647.

182 Berson, Y., & Avolio, B.J. (2004). 'Transformational leadership and the dissemination of organizational goals: A case study of a telecommunication firm.' *The Leadership Quarterly*, 15(5), 625-646.

183 Awamleh, R., & Gardner, W. L. (1999). 'Perceptions of leader charisma and effectiveness: The effects of vision content, delivery, and organizational performance.' *The Leadership Quarterly*, 10, 345–373.

184 Brown, M. E., Treviño, L. K., & Harrison, D. A. (2005). 'Ethical leadership: A social learning perspective for construct development and testing.' *Organizational Behavior and Human Decision Processes*, 97, 117–134.

185 Treviño & Nelson, K.A. (2003). 'Managing business ethics.' Wiley.

186 Ariely, D. (2009). 'Predictably irrational: The hidden forces that shape our decisions.' HarperCollins.

187 Howell, J.M., & Shamir, B. (2005). 'The role of followers in the charismatic leadership process: Relationships and their consequences.' *Academy of Management Review*, 30, 96–112.

188 Steffens, N.K., & Haslam, S.A. (2013). 'Power through "Us": Leaders' use of we-referencing language predicts election victory.' *PLos ONE*, 8(10), 1-6.

189 Mayer, R. C., Davis, J. H., & Schoorman, F. D. (1995). 'An integrative model of organizational trust.' *Academy of Management Review*, 20(3), 709–734.

190 Rousseau, D. M., Sitkin, S. B., Burt, R. S., & Camerer, C. (1998). 'Not so different after all: A cross-discipline view of trust.' *Academy of Management Review*, 23, 393-404.

191 Colquitt, J. A., Scott, B. A., & LePine, J. A. (2007). 'Trust, trustworthiness, and trust propensity: A meta-analytic test of their unique relationships with risk taking and job performance.' *Journal of Applied Psychology*, 92, 909–927.

192 De Cremer, D., & Tyler, T. R. (2007). 'The effects of trust in authority and procedural fairness on cooperation.' *Journal of Applied Psychology*, 92, 639–649.

193 Pillutla, M. M., Malhotra D., & Murnighan, J. K. (2003). 'Attributions of trust and the calculus of reciprocity.' *Journal of Experimental Social Psychology*, 39(5), 448-455.

194 Mayer, R. C., Davis, J. H., & Schoorman, F. D. (1995). 'An integrative model of organizational trust.' *Academy of Management Review*, 20(3), 709–734.

195 van Knippenberg, D.van Ginkel, W.P. & Homan, A.C. 2013. 'Diversity mindsets and the performance of diverse teams.' *Organizational Behavior and Human Decision Processes*, 121(2), 183-193.

196 Boyatzis, R.E., Passarelli, A.M, Koenig, K., Lowe, M., Mathew, B., Stoller, J.K., & Phillips, M. (2012). 'Examination of the neural substrates activated in memories of experiences with resonant and dissonant leaders.' *The Leadership Quarterly*, 23(2), 259-272.

197 Qiu, T., Qualls, W., Bohlmann, J., & Rupp, D.E. (2009). 'The effect of interactional fairness on the performance of cross-functional product development teams: A multi-level mediated model.' *The Journal of Product Innovation Management*, 26(2), 173-187.

198 McKinsey (2018). 'Skill shift: Automation and the future of the workforce.' Retrieved from: https://www.mckinsey.com/~/media/McKinsey/Featured%20Insights/Future%20of%20Organizations/Skill%20shift%20Automation%20and%20the%20future%20of%20the%20workforce/MGI-Skill-Shift-Automation-and-future-of-the-workforce-May-2018.ashx

199 Ou, A.Y., Waldman, D.A., & Peterson, S.J. (2006). 'Do humble CEO's matter? An examination of CEO humility and firm outcomes.' *Journal of Management*, 44(3), 1147-1173.

200 Vera, D., & Rodriguez-Lopez, A. (2004). 'Humility as a source of competitive advantage.' *Organizational Dynamics*, 33(4), 393-408.

201 Owens, B.P., Johnson, M.D., & Mitchell, T.R. (2013). 'Expressed humility in organizations: Implications of performance, teams and leadership.' *Organization Science*, 24(5), 1517-1538.

202 McKinsey (September 2019). 'Catch them if you can: How leaders in data and analytics have pulled ahead.' Retrieved from: https://www.mckinsey.com/business-functions/mckinsey-analytics/our-insights/catch-them-if-you-can-how-leaders-in-data-and-analytics-have-pulled-ahead

Chapter 10

203 Friedman, M. (1970). 'The social responsibility of business is to increase its profits.' *The New York Times Magazine*, September 13.

204 De Cremer, D. (2018). 'Why Mark Zuckerberg's Leadership Failure was a Predictable Surprise.' *The European Business Review*, May-June, 7-10.

205 Darwin, C. (2006). *On the Origin of Species*. Dover Publications Inc.

206 PwC (2018). 'PwC data uncovers disconnect between C-suite perception and employee experience with workplace technology.' Retrieved from: https://www.pwc.com/us/en/press-releases/2018/c-suite-perception-employee-experience-disconnect.html

207 Accenture (2018). 'The big disconnect: AI, leaders and the workforce.' Retrieved from: https://www.accenture.com/us-en/insights/future-workforce/big-disconnect-ai-leaders-workforce and Accenture report (2018). Realizing the full value of AI. Retrieved from: https://www.accenture.com/_acnmedia/pdf-77/accenture-workforce-banking-survey-report

208 Microsoft (2019). Microsoft – IDC Study: Artificial Intelligence to nearly double the rate of innovation in Asia Pacific by 2021. https://news.microsoft.com/apac/2019/02/20/microsoft-idc-study-artificial-intelligence-to-nearly-double-the-rate-of-innovation-in-asia-pacific-by-2021/

209 Boston Consulting Group (2019). 'The death and life of management.' Retrieved from: https://www.bcg.com/d/press/18september2019-life-and-death-of-management-229539

210 Maack, M.M. (2019). 'Youtube recommendations are toxic, says dev who worked on the algorithm.' Retrieved from: https://thenextweb.com/google/2019/06/14/youtube-recommendations-toxic-algorithm-google-ai/

211 Mitchell, M. (2019). 'Artificial Intelligence: A guide for thinking humans.' Farrar, Straus and Giroux.

212 Davies, B. Diemand-Yauman, C., & van Dam, N. (2019). 'Competitive advantage with a human dimension: From lifelong learning to lifelong employability.' *McKinsey Quarterly*, February 2019. Retrieved from: https://www.mckinsey.com/featured-insights/future-of-work/competitive-advantage-with-a-human-dimension-from-lifelong-learning-to-lifelong-employability

213 *The Wall Street Journal* (2019). 'Amazon to retrain a third of its U.S. Workforce.' Retrieved from: https://www.wsj.com/articles/amazon-to-retrain-a-third-of-its-u-s-workforce-11562841120

214 Microsoft. AI Business School. Retrieved from: https://www.microsoft.com/en-us/ai/ai-business-school

215 Wiener, N. (1960). 'Some moral and technical consequences of automation.' *Science*, 131(3410), 1355-1358.

216 Vasquez, Z. (2018). 'The truth about killer robots: The year's most terrifying documentary.' Retrieved from: https://www.theguardian.com/film/2018/nov/26/the-truth-about-killer-robots-the-years-most-terrifying-documentary

217 *The Economist* (2019). 'There are no killer robots yet – but regulators must respond to AI in 2019.' Retrieved from: https://www.economist.com/the-world-in/2018/12/17/there-are-no-killer-robots-yet-but-regulators-must-respond-to-ai-in-2019

218 Smith, B. (2018). 'Facial recognition: It's time for action.' Retrieved from: https://blogs.microsoft.com/on-the-issues/2018/12/06/facial-recognition-its-time-for-action/

Index

M

N

O

P

CPSIA information can be obtained
at www.ICGtesting.com
Printed in the USA
LVHW021204300620
659260LV00006B/9

9 780857 198280